The Power of Language in the Clinical Process

Assessing and Treating the Bilingual Person

RoseMarie Pérez Foster, Ph.D.

JASON ARONSON INC.
Northvale, New Jersey
London

Production Editor: Elaine Lindenblatt

This book was set in 11 pt. New Baskerville and printed and bound by Book-mart Press, Inc. of North Bergen, NJ.

Library of Congress Cataloging-in-Publication Data

Foster, RoseMarie Pérez.
    The power of language in the clinical process : Assessing and treating the bilingual person / RoseMarie Pérez Foster.
      p. cm.
    Includes bibliographical references and index.
    ISBN 0-7657-0179-0
    1. Psychiatry, Transcultural. 2. Bilingualism—Psychological aspects. 3. Psychotherapy patients—Language. I. Title.
    [DNLM: 1. Mental Disorders—therapy. 2. Communication Barriers. 3. Multilingualism. WM 400 F756a 1999]
    RC455.4.E8F67 1999
    616.89—DC21
    DNLM/DLC
    for Library of Congress   98–7632

Printed in the United States of America on acid-free paper. For information and catalog write to Jason Aronson Inc., 230 Livingston Street, Northvale, NJ 07647-1726. Or visit our website: http://www.aronson.com

To Jeff, Lauren, James and Patria
and
Ramón, Alberto, Chefito, y Rafael:

desaparecidos pero no olvidados

Contents

PART III: TREATING THE BILINGUAL PERSON

Acknowledgments

As an immigrant daughter and clinician, I am indebted to those immigrants of New York City who, through the venues of Roosevelt, Mount Sinai, Bellevue, and Creedmore Hospitals, multiple community settings, and private consulting rooms, have permitted me entry into their multiple-language worlds.

This book could not have been possible without the support and vision of my friend, colleague, and publisher at Jason Aronson Inc.: Michael Moskowitz. His focus toward diversifying the ethnocentric base of the mental health literature will serve as a significant influence in the shape of our knowledge. Thanks to Drisdy Kee, my assistant, for her persistence, dedication, and kindness throughout the preparation of this manuscript. And finally my deepest thanks go to Jeff Foster, my partner in life, whose support and love have always kept my work in perspective.

RM. P. F.

PART I

INTRODUCING THE BILINGUAL MIND

1

Bilingual People
in Clinical Treatment

The last decade has seen the publication of an unprecedented number of practice-oriented volumes that address the role of cultural diversity in the clinical process. Works such as *Ethnicity and Family Therapy* (McGoldrick et al. 1982), *Cross-Cultural Mental Health* (Comas-Diaz and Griffith 1988), *Counseling the Culturally Different* (Sue and Sue 1990), *The Analyst in the Inner City* (Altman 1995), as well as *Reaching Across Boundaries of Culture and Class: Widening the Scope of Psychotherapy*, which I co-edited with Michael Moskowitz and Rafael Art. Javier (Pérez Foster et al. 1996e), are representative of the "ethnic turn" recently taken by the mental health and social service professions. As providers in increasingly diverse urban centers, clinicians must address their anxieties and inadequacies as they attempt to do clinical work with people whose cultural worlds so markedly differ from their own. The ethnic shift in the field is both ethically driven and long overdue, as practitioners face the shameful fact that ethnically diverse individuals, when treated in American institutions, are frequently misdiagnosed, relegated to less competent clinicians, and subject to clinical biases by their therapists (Atkinson 1985, Sue 1988, Sue and Sue 1990).

Something is clearly wrong with a service profession that possesses limited knowledge and technique in rendering service to a large segment of its clients. Recent critiques of current practice methods have unsparingly pointed to the Western ethnocentric biases in the theoretical assumptions that inform current practice methods (Guernaccia 1993, Sue and Sue 1990). Furthermore, theorists and clinicians alike are beginning to examine the psychodevelopmental constructs that define the American view of psychological health, and establish the goals of wellness for its therapeutic interventions (Bruner 1986, Cushman 1990, Kirschner 1990, Pérez Foster 1993b).

This volume is intended as a hopeful addition to the new field of knowledge on clinical assessment and treatment of foreign-born individuals who present for mental health treatment in the United States. More specifically, this work will attempt to integrate both academic and clinical knowledge in an area that has received negligible attention in the ethnically focused practice literature: the intervening role of *language* per se and *bilingualism* in the personality functioning, symptom formation, and clinical process of ethnic clients. Bilingual individuals enter our institutions, agencies, and consulting rooms and, for the most part, communicate their distress in English, their second language. This is an idiom that is far removed from their early formative experiences, their current daily lives at home, and possibly their emotional inner selves, as well. As problem-focused practitioners trained to define and evaluate symptomatic distress and develop therapeutic interventions, we have naively assumed that verbal fluency in a second language represents lockstep translation of an experience (distant or recent) "lived" in the native tongue. We have also assumed that, for the bilingual person, languages function as interchangeable verbal modules for the expression of the same ideas. Aside from a rare few, mental health practitioners have rarely considered the fact that language is both a unique expressor of meaning for the culture it represents, and a dynamic force within the psyche which can be used to variously express different aspects of the self.

Thus, for the ethnic patient who is a proficient English speaker: Do we assume that their responses to diagnostic queries represent the full spectrum of affective and cognitive experience? Or might certain psychological processes be best represented through the native idiom? And what of the clinical process; are we sure that a psychotherapy conducted in a second language can adequately reconstruct and repair early developmental trauma experienced in a native language? Or must real healing be processed through the affect-laden idiom of the actual events? And what of the nonproficient English speaker? How does a clinician adequately assess the psychological state of a person who has a poor command of the therapist's language? How does a practitioner meaningfully discern the relationship between a client's affective experience and his or her verbal narrative, when so much psychic effort is being deflected onto the demands of translation and the encumbrances of limited vocabulary?

These are pivotal and, in my view, ethically driven questions for any practitioner who works with ethnically diverse clients. However, a meaningful attempt to respond to them will necessarily lead us to even more basic issues: the phenomenon of multiple language acquisition, its dynamic role in psychological development, and its relationship to the organization and expression of lived experience. For the practitioner who treats bilingual people, this volume will essentially function as a clinically focused psycholinguistic handbook on bilingualism.

Part I, "Introducing the Bilingual Mind," describes the developmental and operational dynamics of the bilingual mind, exploring its impact on the psyche through information generated from various disciplinary spheres. While many of the clinical and academic concerns of this volume will apply to multiple-language speakers, the formal presentation and discussion of literature is focused on those academic and clinical reports that have studied bilingual speakers. Part II, "Assessing the Bilingual Person," guides the practitioner through the important variables that impact on clinical evaluation, and offers approaches to interpretation and assessment that integrate the effects of dual-language functioning on the manifest personality. Part III, "Treating the Bilingual Person," presents the complex psychodynamic and technical factors involved in working with a person in their non-native language. It offers specific clinical interventions for this situation and guides the practitioner in their use through case examples and discussion.

POSING THE CLINICAL ISSUES

We are in the midst of massive shifts in worldwide migration patterns (Desjarlais et al. 1995). The United States, the traditional recipient of those who seek a safe haven in the diaspora, received 915,900 legal immigrants in 1996 (United States Immigration and Naturalization Service 1997). The 1990 census attempted some estimates of the current bilingual population in the United States and found that approximately 40 percent speak a non-English native language. For the mental health field, these figures represent the proportionally increasing number of foreign-born people who will seek services for psychological distress in American social service and mental health institutions. These will be clients whose mother tongue is not American English, and who possess some form of bilingualism—from English learned upon arrival in the United States, or from study in their own countries. In this volume, I am operationally using an open-ended definition of bilingualism that is favored by linguists such as Hakuta (1986) and Haugen (1953). This broad definition views the bilingual person as a speaker of one language who can understand and make themselves understood in the complete and meaningful utterances of another language. I use the terms *balanced* or *proficient bilingual* throughout this book to denote a fairly equal verbal fluency in both languages. There are further distinctions within bilingualism that will be defined and discussed later on in the volume.

Bilingual people who present for treatment will of course span a wide spectrum of characteristics, including age, level of acculturation, socioeconomic status, education, skills training, length of stay in the United States, and mental status. They might include a frightened Salvadoran youth who has been sent to the United States to escape military induction, a Chinese exchange student who is too depressed to leave his dorm, a Russian man in Brighton Beach whose panic attacks no longer allow him to drive his cab, a Liberian refugee whose family was massacred in a civil war, an aphasic Greek woman who has lived in Washington Heights for fifty years, or an Italian psychotherapist who has never used his native language since he arrived in New York as a child. These immigrants, who represent very different levels of acculturation to American life, may function with varying levels of proficiency in the English-speaking everyday world, but in spontaneous moments may sing, curse in anger, soothe a child, hallucinate, count their money, dream, or make love all in their mother tongue. These pointed verbal actions tap at the quick of their emotional lives; however, their soulful meanings would probably be lost if translated to a language that is removed from the sensual context of the lived experience (Pérez Foster 1996d). Indeed, the mother language has been described in the psycho-analytic literature as the repository of our most basic desires, and the language system which holds the fullest complement of sensorial, affective, and cognitive elements related to early experience (Amahti-Mehler et al. 1993, Buxbaum 1949, Greenson 1950, Loewald 1980).

The question thus begs to be asked: Can mental health treatment offered in a patient's second language—even when the patient is optimally fluent—tap at the meaningful levels of inner experience so central to many psychotherapies? Upon seeking mental-health services, bilingual immigrants present their problems in living, and clinicians attempt to understand their distress via the meaning systems of their own American culture and language. But in fact, how good a job are we doing? For besides needing to integrate migration and acculturation factors with their clients' presenting complaints, clinicians must also consider the covarying influence of their clients' bilingual status. These are people who possess more than one language system through which they can think about themselves, express ideas, and interact with the people in their world. This duality is a unique characteristic of bilinguals, one which must surely impact on how they go about narrating their distress and life story in the treatment process.

Though not carefully recorded, the phenomenon of bilingualism has probably exerted its influences on the mental health field since its inception. Freud was a monolingual German speaker who conducted his early treatments with many patients who were not native German speakers. They included French, Russian, and American patients who underwent analysis with him using their secondarily acquired German (Flegenheimer 1989, Menaker 1989, personal communication 1992). It was not until 1949 and 1950 that the first reports appeared on the potential problems inherent in treating patients in their second language. Buxbaum (1949) and Greenson (1950), two German-and-English-speaking bilingual psychoanalysts working in the United States, proposed that conducting treatment in a patient's second language might render certain areas of the patient's psyche unavailable to the therapy. This was due, they suggested, to the material's independence from the language system in which the treatment was being conducted. In 1955, Kraph, a multilingual psychoanalyst working and reporting from Argentina, elaborated on the idea that the polyglot's choice of language in analysis—when given the option to switch because of the therapist's multilingualism—was often motivated by the patient's anxiety. Kraph reported several examples of patients shifting to the language which aroused the least amount of emotional intensity and disruption.

Substantive exploration of these fascinating clinical observations was not pursued until the 1970s. The new contributors to this literature, who comprise only a fairly small number, have sought to expand on the *experiential unavailability* theme, as well as to describe the role that bilingualism plays on anxiety reduction, symptom formation, defensive structures, memory functions, diagnostic assessment, and the treatment process per se (Amati-Mehler 1993, Aragno and Schlachet 1996, Flegenheimer 1989, Javier 1989, 1995, 1996, Marcos 1972, 1976, Marcos and Alpert 1976, Marcos et al. 1973a, Marcos and Urcuyo 1979, Pérez Foster 1992, 1996a,b,c, Rozensky and Gomez 1983). Although offering consistent support for the important intervening role that language plays in the bilingual person's psychic processes, this literature remains extremely unrefined in its clinical practice recommendations with this type of patient. Furthermore, the field has not sufficiently integrated the wealth of information on bilingualism that has begun to emerge from other disciplines.

Paralleling the mental health field's renewed interests in bilingualism has been the recent surge of interest in language studies emerging from other academic perspectives. From developmental psycholinguistics comes a fresh view of the language learning process as a dialectical enterprise that is embedded within the matrix of human relationships (Dore 1979, Halliday 1975, Nelson 1990, Stern 1985). From semiotic theory emerges a focus on the human narrative, and a view of interactional discourse as an activity that bursts with meanings, symbols, and guideposts for living in the sociocultural surround (Kristeva 1980, Lacan 1977). These perspectives hold much promise for the student of bilingual phenomena, for they point to the key role of social relationships in the development of language meaning. In addition, I also view this work as underlining the notion that a bilingual person's differential language use may evoke elements of the human relational and social context within which the speaker's respective languages were acquired. Both developmental and psychodynamically oriented clinicians might thus be moved to consider that different languages, when learned in a separate context within unique object relationships and conditions, might later evoke distinct object-related venues of self experience and self-expression (Pérez Foster 1992, 1996a).

Finally, the last two decades have also seen a surge of cognitive and neurologic inquiry into the general topography, if you will, of the bilingual mind. This research literature has reported complex and compelling evidence suggesting that bilingual persons who have learned their languages in different developmental contexts may store portions of their languages in separate organizational systems in the brain. These systems are purported to maintain parallel encoding mechanisms, such that each language code has its own stream of associations between meaning and experiential events stored in the ideational system (Jakobovits and Lambert 1961, Kolers 1963, Lambert et al. 1958, Lambert and Moore 1966, Ojemann and Whitaker 1978, Paradis 1978,

1980b). Known as the *language independence phenomenon*, this suggested duality in the neurorepresentation and cognitive organization of language holds key interest for clinicians. At the very least it opens the question of a potential duality in the bilingual patient's projected narrative of internal concerns in the treatment process. On a deeper level, it stirs a fascinating and complex set of issues regarding the role of language in general psychic organization.

Having posed numerous developmental, clinical, and practice issues that need to be considered in treating the bilingual client, I would like to proceed in the following chapters of Part I of this book to elaborate an operational picture of the bilingual mind. In order to do this I will traverse the discourse of multiple clinical theoretical perspectives, and discuss the relevant databases that emerge from several academic disciplines. However, my aim is very specific: *to comprehensively integrate the multidisciplinary literature on bilingualism for the clinician*. It is time that the parameter of language be finally considered in the clinical assessment and treatment of the ever-diversifying ethnic client populations that seek our mental health services.

2

The Dynamics of Speech in Developmental Processes

This chapter takes on the formidable task of introducing the clinical practitioner to what I term the living dynamics of speech. Despite our daily consumption of language as the basic stock in trade of our profession, American mental health practitioners are narrowly educated in the domain of language phenomena. As diagnosticians and psychotherapists we have been trained in one focal dimension of language activity: its capacity to represent interior psychic processes. For the most part, we view verbalization as a mere conduit for mental operations, as opposed to a dynamic operation which can carve out segments of reality as well as shape the meaning of experience.

For us in the mental-health professions, Freud merely scratched the surface of language when he nevertheless impressively described the potency of both its manifest and latent meaning functions. Subsequent students of language who have attempted to understand its complex dialectical connection with both interior psychological processes and the external world have variously described language as a cultural template for organizing the world (Sapir 1929), a reflector of the social order (Vygotsky 1978), an illusionary evoker of human presence (Anzieu 1983), a symbolic capsule of deep desire (Lacan 1977), and a mutative agent in the elaboration of the self (Harris 1992). For the clinician, the relevance of these dynamic language operations to the dual-language mind, is that given the intrinsic role of culture in language-making, they begin to speak for the possible existence of dual systems of symbolic meaning for naming and interpreting the world and signifying the self.

Hakuta (1986) points out that the fascinating thing about the bilingual mind is how it goes about interfacing two parallel code systems, which must somehow both cooperate and compete to coexist within a single mental system. As we will see in subsequent chapters, Hakuta's interface is of significance to us. While he was referring to dual-language interaction from a cognitive and information-processing perspective, the clinical literature has essentially been reporting its own observations of the dual-language interface, noting that dual-language interaction also seems to be mediated by *psychodynamic processes*. For example, a bilingual child's developmental experiences may have commanded particular language choices for specific interpersonal experiences (Russian with mother; English with father). Or specific functional or contextual domains may have demanded particular language choices for the child (Spanish for home, English for school). Linguists have considered these language acquisition and early usage patterns in bilingual persons from the perspective of functional separations in the bilingual's two languages (Lambert et al. 1958, Taylor 1971), as well as the contexts that cue language choices (Ervin-Tripp 1968, Fishman 1965). Psychodynamically oriented clinicians, however, additionally propose that the bilingual's respective languages are deeply intertwined with the internalized representations of the important others who the child learns the languages from. Furthermore, these languages also become integral to the aspects of self experience and expression that evolve within those language-specific object relationships (Pérez Foster 1992, 1996a,b,c, Stern 1985).

On this issue of psychodynamic factors mediating the language interface in bilinguals, the clinical literature further describes that while dual-language speakers make *conscious* language choices depending on the contextual demands of their environments, they also seem to use their bilingualism to *unconsciously* ward off painful language-related segments of previous and current experience. In these situations, the language in which an anxiety-laden situation did *not* take place can become unconsciously enlisted in psychic defensive functions, and can be used to isolate the disturbing complement of emotions associated with traumatic events. Thus the sudden deaths of a French-American woman's siblings, when she was a child, can be recounted by her with significantly less anguish and disorganizing anxiety in English than in her native French.

These fascinating clinical processes will be fully explored in the chapters that follow, but before moving further into the psychodynamics of the bilingual interface and its relevance to the adequate psychological assessment and treatment of bilingual patients, I would first like to lay some conceptual groundwork for the clinician on the living dynamics of language, per se. My aim in this chapter is to convert the clinician from one who listens to words as mere vehicles of internal expression, to one who also views words as dynamic sculptors of experience. From the spheres of psycholinguistics and psychoanalytically informed developmental theory, I have selected a spectrum of conceptual frameworks, each of which represents a unique perspective of dynamic action in the language making process.

LANGUAGE AS THE CULTURAL ORGANIZER OF EXPERIENCE

In the United States, the general public's knowledge of psycholinguistics is generally limited to a phenomenon which tends also to amuse them: that Eskimos have many words in their vocabulary for snow. I include mental health clinicians in this sample of people who may or may not be additionally aware of the fact that the Eskimo culture's more variegated consideration of snow conditions bears a vital connection to the integral role that snow plays in daily life.

In the 1920s, the linguists E. Sapir (1949) and B. Whorf (1956) described the intimate relationship between spoken words and the cultural groups that created them. Emerging at that time from social science's spirited new interests in cultural phenomena (e.g., Malinowski 1926, Mead 1935), they viewed language as a unique expression of how each culture views its own sociocultural surround. A culture's language, they contended, was empowered with the function of focusing on those segments of the physical, interpersonal, and experiential landscape which had unique relevance for life within the group. These linguists of the relativist school (Hakuta 1986), advocated the basic notion that language was not merely a collection of verbal symbols with which people communicate ideas, but rather that symbolic language itself, embedded in its culture, represented the template through which people of a cultural group patterned and organized their environment. According to Sapir, "we as individuals see, hear and experience very largely as we do because the language habits of our community predispose certain choices of interpretation" (1929, p. 209). Following this view, people who have acquired two or more languages from their life and immersion in different cultural communities might reasonably come to possess more than one template through which to linguistically organize their experiential worlds.

In the Spanish-speaking Caribbean, there is a name for the simultaneous changes in light, humidity, temperature, and atmospheric aroma that take place when darkness begins to fall. The word *sereno* describes the purple duskiness, dry chill, and change in sea and soil smells at this time of day. For children in some rural areas, *sereno* is a cue for the time to come in from outdoor games and avoid the first rumblings of the spirit world that come to life after full darkness. For menstruating young girls, *sereno* also means taking shelter from the sudden change in temperature and humidity that can influence their temporarily unstable constitutions. *Sereno* has no corresponding word and, most important, no necessary place in—for example—the urban English-speaking landscape. However, one sees the cultural power and highly condensed meaning of this word in its own socioenvironmental locale, as it selects particular elements from the wide experiential environment and corrals them into a language symbol. Cultural worlds, as pithily described by Schweder (1990), "are intentionally populated with the products of their own design" (p. 75). For Sapir (1949) and Whorf (1956), words name those cultural products—their meanings imparted to the child during the process of language acquisition.

LANGUAGE AS SONOROUS PRESENCE AND TRANSITIONAL PHENOMENON

Even prior to the child's acquisition of language, that is, learning the symbolic word meanings for the products of its culture (Schweder 1990), the child has lived amidst the aural, sensorial productions of its familial surround. This presymbolic dimension of speech—the sensual underbelly of speech activity, as it were—plays an integral role in the infant's early language life. It is first conveyed to the infant by the caretaker's voice in an all-encompassing way—by the mother in the feeding situation, and in all her other ministrations to the child. Her words as such are an undifferentiated audial flow, but the sounds and rhythms of her speech are an accentuating and integral part of her *being with* the child (Loewald 1976). Anzieu (1983) has described the primary caretaker's voice as a sonorous wrapping which envelops the child in a sea of sounds. From a perspective reminiscent of Winnicott's (1951, 1986) conception of transitional space, Anzieu views the infant's early auditory sphere as an audial psychic space through which the baby begins both to differentiate between audial self and other, and likewise to engage in the sonorous illusion of conjuring the mother's presence through sound. When viewed from a Winnicottian perspective, the experience of hearing another's voice, from infancy throughout the life course, probably stands as the most pervasive and consistent transitional phenomenon of all!

The infant's early capacity for experiencing the sensory aspects of language is neither the global, diffuse reaction postulated by early thinkers, nor a primitive, developmental way-station designed to atrophy on its trajectory toward symbolic word formation. Indeed, the infant's capacity for sensorial-auditory discrimination is neurologically quite articulated at birth. Neonates are capable of discriminating and showing preference for their mother's voice fifteen hours after birth (DeCasper and Fifer 1980), and can distinguish their own cry from that of another infant at twenty-four hours (Martin and Clark 1982). Furthermore, through stunningly early recognition of the prosodic characteristics of speech, 4-day-old infants can distinguish utterances in their native languages from those of another language (Mehler et al. 1988). This nascent sensorial capacity of the infant, when coupled with affective states, has been repeatedly shown to constitute the primary organizational cornerstone of early intersubjective communication and experience (Stern 1985, Tronick et al. 1979). This capacity evolves over time, integrates cross-modal sensorial experiences (auditory, visual, tactile, kinesthetic), and, with the advent of language acquisition, is enlisted in symbolic operations. Bucci (1994, 1997) has recently emphasized the role of what she calls perceptual channels as distinct elements in the storage of early memory. By the time of the child's entry into nursery school, he or she can impressively integrate the sensorial qualities of speech with its semantic word meaning, overlaying a speech command, for example, with its physical tone, cadence, and rhythm to form a rather complex message interpretation (Bruner 1981). To this point, every psychodynamically oriented clinician is well aware of the evocative power of physical speech to soothe, stimulate, frighten, or inform, and the intimate association that this speech often bears to early internalized object representations. This sensorial dimension of language—Anzieu's "sonorous ambience" (1983, p. 76)— is perceived by the child from birth, maintained across development, and ultimately integrated with the symbolic meanings of word symbols. As I will expand upon in a later chapter, bilingual speakers in the treatment situation can control immersion into the sonorous ambience of their early language world by using a language in treatment that was acquired at a later stage of development. The mother's tongue has been documented by many bilingual clinicians as holding not only the semantic accuracy of early developmental discourse, but also the sensual sea of sounds that once enveloped the child in the process of her care.

LANGUAGE AS EXPANDER OF SOCIAL EXPERIENCE AND CONDENSER OF DESIRE

For developing children, the onset of formal language operations carries tremendous significance, both for the *intra*personal life of their psychic interior, and the *inter*personal life within their sociocultural surround. Newly trained in the verbal symbols and meaning systems of their particular cultural milieu, children's capacity for social experience now veritably explodes with possibilities. The acquisition of an ever-growing vocabulary of cultural meanings guarantees both the possibility of interpersonal interaction with others, and the currency needed for membership in the society at large. With language, the child enters the social order and acquires the templates through which its culture parses, organizes, and interprets its world (Sapir 1929, Schweder 1991).

As first articulated by Vygotsky (1962, 1978), the initial acquisition of language, as well as other conceptual abilities, takes place within the relational matrix of the child–caretaker dyad. Just as in the earlier presymbolic period where the child and caretaker used the sensorial domain to stimulate and influence each other in the pursuit of intersubjective communication, so do the dyad partners now strive to be together in the new shared experience of verbal symbols. This is a sharing of lingual meanings that have been mutually created by them in their small, two-person society. These are meanings about personal interactions, the external world, and—of great importance to the developing child—verbal meaning labels about their own self-experiences ("You are tired" or "You are happy"). As every child moves beyond the primary caretakers, he or she will engage in further dialectics throughout development. Other members of the child's culture at large will become the new mediators and new verbal negotiators of experience. They will contribute to the further layering and complexity of language meaning (Pérez Foster 1996a, Stern 1985, Wilson and Weinstein 1990), and afford the child ever-new possibilities for interaction and communication.

However, psychoanalytic theorists have also noted (Hartmann 1964, Lacan 1977) that, in tandem with the child's momentous entry into the *exterior* social order through language, there is a parallel process simultaneously developing within the layers of the child's psychic *interior.* It was Freud who originally elaborated the notion of the unconscious as a deep repository of instinctual passion (Freud 1900). This repository was by definition silent, inscrutable, and inextricably bound to pure experience. The deep desire to be merged with the loved one, the physical resonance of bodily pleasure, the ruthless rage of thwarted passion—these were deep experiences unavailable to speech, which lived within the child prior to the encroachments of language and the circumscriptions of the social order (Bowie 1991, Lacan 1977). With the child's linguistic entry into the world, an evolving set of culturally constructed parameters and interdictions begins to invade the recesses of the child's inner life. For the acquisition of word representations, while powerful in their ability to expand the child's interactive involvement with the social world, also introduces the limits to experiential expression through the culture's specialized symbolic word meanings. And this process serves to constrict, contrive, and obfuscate access to the experiential inner world. Lacan (1977) viewed language as a complex layering of word representations which were but oblique, obtuse references to pure inner desire. Word representations belong to the conscious interface with the external world, and though they become highly cathected in psychic life, they inevitably pale against the passion of felt inner experience. Words, Lacan contended, in their powerful ability to contain and operationally titrate the expression of desire, could thus function to maintain order in the social world.

American clinicians of the ego psychology school, such as Hartmann (1964) and Loewenstein (1956), have similarly emphasized the binding capacities of language processes and their ability to forestall the expression of impulse life. Most recently Schafer (1980), in his descriptions of "action language," has elaborated on the sophisticated machinations of language use in adults, and its capacity to maintain the passionate depths of real experience unavailable to the conscious, social surface.

From a cognitive developmental perspective, Stern (1985) has likewise been addressing the "constricting" aspects of language dynamics in his recent descriptions of the child's developing sense of a verbal self. Focusing on the normative course of initial language acquisition, he notes how the new ability for language-making serves to condense, contain, and essentially collapse a myriad of similar lived experiences into the symbol of a single word. Thus, contained within the child's new acquisition of the word symbol *sun*, for example, is the bright light that enters her room in the morning, the light stripes that form when her crib slats make shadows on the wall, the blinding glare in front of her eyes when her swing goes up in the park, the thing in the sky that makes her skin feel warm at the beach, and so on. Words, indeed, are but pale representations of the breadth of our experiences!

Viewed from these perspectives, the acquisition of language heralds the development of multiple operations in the individual. It not only equips individuals with the symbolic currency for successful and consensual social exchange; but, because of this, it also constricts the full expression of their experiences. Furthermore, words, as templates for the cultural environment, further organize, and ascribe meanings to that experiential world, training the individual in certain choices of experiential interpretation. Pertinent to our concerns here are the complex cultural and linguistic vectors that impact upon the speaker of two languages. Especially relevant, but not exclusive to the individual who has learned their languages from life and immersion in different cultural contexts, is the factor of an additional set of symbolic meanings for their experiences. Psycholinguistic research shows that conceptual words such as *loyalty*, or emotional words such as *love*, when presented to bilinguals in each of their respective languages, generate very different streams of associations, thus projecting in simple fashion what are probably complex differences in cultural meanings (Kolers 1968). These linguistic differences in the definition of human experience and emotion are in fact the subject of a new and growing field of exploration variously known as the *anthropology of emotion* (Lutz and White 1986), *cultural psychology* (Schweder 1990), and *ethnopsychiatry* (Gaines 1992). Shifting the balance away from the early searches for universal imperatives, this new perspective underscores how the wide potential spectrum of human emotion is organized and tagged by the specialized sets of meanings, attributions, and values that are defined by the myriad cultural frameworks in which they are respectively embedded (Guernaccia et al. 1996, Kitayama and Marcus 1994). Thus, one of the problems posed for us as the clinicians who will assess and treat these bilingual speakers lies in the word meanings of our inquiries and clinical practices, which are of course embedded in the North American understanding and framework of emotional distress. Adding further to the language–emotion conundrum for the bilingual speaker is the likelihood that conducting their clinical narrative in a second language will probably even further obfuscate early experience originally symbolized in their native language.

LANGUAGE AS THE VOICE OF SELF AND OTHER

As introduced in the discussions above, the interpersonal and intersocial spheres provide the complex matrices within which language is acquired. These language-generating relational experiences take place in the young child, whose capacity for symbol formation develops at a tremendous pace beginning at the end of the first year of life (Bruner 1981).

In a direction similar to recent trends in contemporary psychodevelopmental theory, where foci have shifted from the study of the instinctual bases of personality development to an emphasis on object relations, psycholinguistic theory has also refocused some of its attention from the more biological view of language as a fairly innate and automatic capacity, to the view that language development is also a process rooted in children's relationships with other people (Edgcumbe 1981, Urwin 1984). Adding to the formidable body of research activity conducted on the Chomskian perspective of innate language structure are the works of Bloom (1973), Bruner (1977, 1981), Dore (1975a, 1975b), Stern (1985), and others. These latter works consistently show that a child's ever-evolving experience with interpersonal events is another essential key to understanding how language is acquired.

Verbal language emerges from an array of prelinguistic, intersubjective modes of communication which include eye contact, facial expression, gesturing, and touch, as well as vocal expression (Edgcumbe 1981) and vocal turn-taking (Beebe et al. 1988). Mother and child engage in pre-stages of conversation: the child learns the impact of its vocalizations through its influence on the caretaker, and mothers tend to interpret indications of need in the child as intentionally communicative acts directed toward them. Bruner (1981) proposes that around the end of the first year, children realize that their own vocalizations can affect another's intentionality, and that sounds have meaning.

As noted earlier, it was Vygotsky whose work, at the early part of this century, emphasized the primacy of the child–caretaker matrix in the development of cognitive abilities (1962). The meaning ascribed to words, and the link between lingual code and a real event in the world, were something that caretaker and child produced in the context of their mutual and shared experiences. Language developed, Vygotsky claimed, from the child's *intra*mental representation of *inter*mental activities between themselves and the important other. The child learns the meanings of words within a process of living, sharing, and creating mutually negotiated meanings for his or her dynamic activities with another person. For example, the child's acquisition of the term *ball* has occurred from the traversal of many interactive moments of experience with the caretaker. The dyad has vary-

ingly rolled, thrown, giggled over, bounced, and lost a ball between them—all in the process of creating a verbal meaning
symbol for these shared *ball* experiences.

In the more complex situation of the child's learning self-
referential or self-descriptive word meanings, one can appreci-
ate the complex set of cues that is involved in these word learn-
ing/negotiating processes—from the child's own proprioceptive
experience of self to the caretaker's subjective perception, projection, and labeling of the child's expressions (Harris 1992,
Pérez Foster 1996a). Adding to the complex layerings, especially
of self-descriptive word meanings, are the multiple intimate relationships that the child will have with important others in the
child's early psychodevelopmental and language-acquisitional life,
each of which will create and negotiate specialized word meanings to describe particular relational experiences between the
child and that respective important other. The interactive moments of experience between child and mother which yield the
words meaning "naughty girl" may be very different from those
experiential interactions in the relationship with a caretaking
grandparent which also yield that term (Stern 1985).

Verbal interactions with primary others, and the shared experiences of negotiating verbal word meanings with them, become the prototypical dialogic discourses that are internalized
by the child (Vygotsky 1988). As the child grows and moves
within the culture and society at large, new figures will become
additional verbal negotiators of experience who, within the context of their relationship with the child, will contribute to the
enhanced complexity of language meaning.

Thus the elaboration of language comprises the mutative influences of psychodevelopmental eras, varied social contexts, and
meaning-producing interactions with important others (Wilson
and Weinstein 1990). Taking an object-relations view of language
acquisition, one might see word meanings as a composite of self–
object interactions and negotiations ripe with the affective, cognitive, and social components that went into their elaboration.
Words are the symbolic object-relational capsules of the past.

They are the voice of self and other. Words are the potential evokers of the early experiences and meanings produced in the child's dyadic union with an important other (Pérez Foster 1996a). In the therapeutic situation, words, as argued here, might in fact be seen as the in situ carriers of the transference! They are the symbolic containers of the self and other at a developmental moment in time. The psychodynamic therapeutic process is unique, in fact, in its ability to return to the early relational contexts of language activity (Valsiner 1988, Wilson 1989, Wilson and Weinstein 1990). Consider for example, the sensual presymbolic states that can be aroused by the simple prosody of the therapist's speech, evoking a time when it was mother's voice who bathed the child in a sea of sounds (Anzieu 1983). Viewed from the perspective of Bucci's (1994) multiple code theory of memory storage, the discourse of the therapeutic situation stimulates both sensorial and symbolic channels of internalized experience. Within the context of the transference, words can also invoke the later symbolic stages in language development, resurrecting original meaning situations (Valsiner 1988) within unique self–object interactions. This can open the treatment process to direct observation of developmental self-states and whatever wishes, conflicts, or defensive functions may have been operational during the word-acquisition process (Wilson and Weinstein 1990).

This juncture brings us to the issues of the bilingual speaker. This individual possesses not only dual sets of culturally driven symbols for referring to internal states and the external world, but also two different chains of meaning-producing self–object interactions and developmental contexts. Whether a second language has been learned in a different environmental context, or in a different developmental period (for example: latency school era, adolescent high school years, adult immigration), or whether a second language has simply been learned in early life from a different caretaker, each language system will represent a separate composite of unique relational and contextual experiences. As we will see in Chapter 3, there is a fascinating research literature that suggests that, at the level of neurocognitive organization, many of the affective and cognitive components of these language-specific experiences are processed and stored in memory along language-specific organizational schema. And at the level of psychodynamic organization, we will see in Chapter 4 how these language-specific relational experiences come to be associated with different modes of being, different modes of interacting with another, and possibly different modes of experiencing oneself.

3

Is There an Organization to the Bilingual Mind?

To begin an exploration of how psychic experience is linguistically represented by a person who possesses more than one language system will require the reader to shift perspective—from the psychosocial dynamics of the language process elaborated in the previous chapter to how linguistic experience is represented in neurocognitive processes. This discussion is by no means meant as an exhaustive exposition of the various disciplinary spheres that have generated knowledge in language operations, but rather is specifically geared toward informing the practitioner about those phenomena that will be helpful in the clinical assessment and treatment of bilingual people.

The basic question of whether bilingual individuals organize their languages separately has been the subject of considerable investigation across several disciplines. For the clinician, this question poses a very relevant set of questions regarding the role of the bilingual's languages in psychic processes: Can events experienced in one language be fully expressed in another language? Do separate language systems imply separate manifest personalities? And what of the linguistic influence on psychological symptoms? The linguistic data that are relevant to these clinical concerns have been generated by neurology, cognitive psychology, psycholinguistics, psychological projective testing, and finally in the clinical setting. The data are substantial and, especially in the area of psycholinguistics, at times controversial. However, they nevertheless suggest that bilingualism plays an intervening role in the organization, recall, and expression of affective and cognitive experience, particularly for those who have learned their two languages in different contextual circumstances at separate times in their lives. I would like to present the reader with a fascinating array of multidisciplinary findings—all of which address some basic aspect of organization or mental representation within the bilingual mind.

NEUROLOGICAL STUDIES

Hilda R. is a 72-year-old bilingual Spanish-English woman who presented in her local hospital emergency room with two symptoms that greatly disturbed her: a blackout spell on the previous day, and losing most of her capacity to speak English, a language she had been fluent in since her high school years. The patient was diagnosed with having suffered a cerebrovascular accident (a stroke), which had left her with an expressive aphasia in one of her languages.

Tu-Ping M., a 49-year-old bilingual Chinese-English speaking man, was admitted to the hospital with a brain aneurysm. The patient was left compromised in motoric and linguistic spheres, with a fairly severe expressive aphasia that impacted both of his languages equally.

Neurology has commonly looked to cases of aphasia, that is, language loss due to cerebrovascular insult, trauma, or deteriorative organic brain syndrome, for information on how language is organized in the brain (Bastion 1984, Brown 1972, Goodglass 1983). Penfield and Roberts's (1959) early comprehensive work in brain language localization showed that over 90 percent of linguistic aphasias resulted from lesions to the left cortical hemisphere. Thus, the question was posed by students of bilingualism: If language is stored in a localized area of the cortex, might not a bilingual person who suffers injury to any area of the language cortex show the same degree of loss for their two languages? Observations of language loss and recovery patterns in bilingual aphasics in fact show that some do lose and recover both their languages at the same rate, as in the case of Tu-Ping M. above. However, a significant segment of bilingual cases, like that of Hilda R., lose and recover their two languages in very different patterns (see Albert and Obler [1978] and Paradis [1977], for extensive reviews of this literature). Some bilinguals recover the first learned language before the second. Others recover the most recently used (pre-trauma) language first. Still others initially recover the language used most frequently in current daily life (Chary 1986). Albert and Obler (1978) have even reported cases of different types of aphasia for each language.

Researchers interpret the findings of differential loss and recovery patterns after brain injury as suggestive of separate linguistic representation and organization at the cortical level of the brain. Paradis (1977) has explained this variability of loss and recovery patterns through a dual system hypothesis. The bilingual's two languages, he proposes, are probably represented in distinct as well as overlapping areas of the brain. Whether or not differential language damage occurs would depend on whether the cortical lesion is in an area where the two languages overlap, or an area where only one language is represented.

These conclusions were later supported by the cortical language-localization work of Ojemann and Whitaker (1978) and Ojemann (1991), who electrostimulated the cortex of bilingual patients undergoing neurosurgery. These authors were able to "map out" cortical areas that were specific for each language, as well as areas in which both languages were represented. At the time of their first report in 1978, the authors suggested that an ideal venue for further investigation would be actual observation of cortical activity in the bilingual speaker during differential language use. In 1997, more than a decade after Ojemann and Whitaker's proposal for this research, Kim et al. (1997) began to report their cortical localization work with bilingual speakers, this time using sophisticated magnetic resonance imaging (MRI) technology which allowed the researchers to observe changes in

blood flow activity to different parts of the language cortex during differential language use. These researchers separated their
subject sample into two groups. They compared cortical language
localization in those bilinguals who had learned their two languages simultaneously in infancy (these persons are termed *compound bilinguals*), with bilinguals who had learned their second
language at a later time in development (termed *coordinate
bilinguals*). As we will see later in this chapter, the reason for
creating these two sampling groups was that earlier studies in
psycholinguistics had indicated the presence of two separate linguistic systems for bilinguals who had learned and become proficient in a second language at a later time in their development
(Ervin and Osgood 1954, Kolers 1963, 1968, Lambert 1956,
Lambert et al. 1958). In their cortical localization studies, Kim
et al. (1997) found cortical areas that were commonly activated
by use of both languages. However, in people who had learned
their languages at two separate times in life, they also found
evidence of cortical activity in areas that were specific for each
language's use. Those who had learned their two languages simultaneously from infancy showed no such cortical area distinctions. The authors viewed this data as implying that, in addition
to the cortical structures that are established at the time of initial language acquisition (whether one or two languages are
learned simultaneously), separate structures will also be generated later to accommodate acquisition of a language learned after
the initial language acquisition era of infancy.

    For clinicians, the finding of differentials in the neural rep-
resentation of language in the brain carries important significance because of its stunning implications for similar differentials in cognitive structure. Also pertinent to our concerns are
issues of psychodevelopment and the "psychic structures" that we
surmise to evolve along the developmental trajectory. The intervening variable of language is now one that must be considered
in psychic structural formation, as will become evident in the
ensuing chapters. And of greatest importance to us are the psychic disturbances that we attempt to assess and treat in the clini-

cal setting. Are they impacted by intervening "bi-linguistic" variables that have heretofore eluded our clinical attention? The concerns aroused by the research reported thus far are formidable: Do our English-language assessment methodologies access the memory stored in both language systems proposed for the coordinate bilingual? This is the bilingual person who has learned his or her two languages separately, and who is essentially represented by our immigrant clients. And finally, simply stated: Does treatment in one language reconstruct the full life story, even if there is equal proficiency in both languages? In the attempt to grapple with these disturbing questions, I will move on to the work of other investigative perspectives which will hopefully shed further light on these phenomena.

PSYCHOLINGUISTIC EVIDENCE

The exploration of differences in the neural representation of languages in the brain is paralleled by investigations in psycholinguistics and cognitive psychology that have been exploring potential differences in the cognitive organization of dual-language systems. Working from the perspective of information-processing approaches to human cognition, investigators have been interested in studying how different language codes are connected to conceptual meaning, and the various phases involved as these respective codes are processed from original acquisition; through storage in memory; to subsequent retrieval and usage (Ervin and Osgood 1954, Kolers 1963, 1968, Lambert 1956, Lambert et al. 1958, Macnamara 1967).

The years from the 1950s to the 1970s saw avid research and debate in the psycholinguistic literature on the distinction between *compound* and *coordinate* bilingualism. This was the idea that there existed qualitatively different types of proficient bilingual speakers who organized their languages in different types of cognitive structures. Initially proposed by the linguist Weinreich (1953), this notion was investigated experimentally and revised by Ervin and Osgood (1954). These were cognitive

psychologists who became interested in the developmental contexts which produced different types of bilingual speakers.

It was the contention of the compound-coordinate distinction that separate language acquisition contexts would enhance
the functional separation of the bilingual's two languages in
memory, while acquisition in fused contexts would reduce functional separation. The compound bilingual was optimally represented by the person who had learned (and interchanged usage
of) two languages from early childhood. These speakers had a
single set of representational meanings for which they simply
possessed two different language symbols. The coordinate
bilinguals, on the other hand, had learned their second language
at a different developmental period and in a different environmental context (school, work, immigrant country, etc.)
(Genessee 1978). This bilingual group possessed two different
sets of representational meaning systems in memory, each with
its own respective language symbol. Using mainly word-association protocols and examining such characteristics as associational
content, language interaction, and word satiation phenomena,
the research of this time reported many results consistent with
the hypothesis that coordinate bilinguals had language systems
that were organized independently of each other (Grosjean 1982,
Jakobovits and Lambert 1961, Kolers 1968, Lambert et al. 1958).
The research infers that these bilinguals maintain parallel encoding systems, such that each language has its own stream of associations, that is, meanings between words and experiential events
stored in the memory system.

The obvious implications of these findings for the bilingual
person in treatment, especially the immigrant patient who in all
probability has learned his or her second language in a different developmental or environmental context, has never been
integrated in the body of clinical practice literature. The idea
that a clinical treatment could be conducted in a second language—a language system that has a different neurological representation, cognitive organization, and set of meanings from
that language system in which developmental experiences were

first coded and organized—is rather stunning! This does indeed force us to wonder about the bilingual's use of the second language in the clinical process.

COGNITION AND MEMORY STUDIES

Early cognition research in laboratory settings showed the presence of language differentials in bilinguals' memory organization and recall of experience. The works of Brown and Lennenberg (1954), Ervin (1961), and others indicated that language affects the classification of stimuli and its subsequent recall in memory. This information and its impressive clinical implications were only very recently brought to light, when Javier and colleagues (1993) and Javier (1996) started to explore the interaction between bilingualism and memory in the clinical situation. These authors studied proficient bilinguals' recollection and description of an autobiographical event in both their respective languages. Personal events recalled by subjects in the language in which events were actually experienced (whether this was the native or secondarily acquired language) showed different content organization, enhanced detail, and greater textural vividness than when the same events were recalled in the subjects' other language. Laren's (1997) recent study of early memory narratives in coordinate bilinguals emphasized the unique relationship between the use of the early developmental language and its ability to access the complex multimodal elements of that historical era. She found, in addition, that this greater access to experiential detail was also accompanied by heightened affective arousal, an observation which has marked implications for the working through of trauma in the treatment process.

At issue here for the clinician of course is the question of how fully the cognitive, affective, imagistic, and symbolic elements of early formative experiences can be reconstructed in the clinical situation, in a language that did not originally encode those events. In clinical treatment, considering the spectrum of psychodynamic determinants that we already know to be involved in repressive mechanisms (Freud 1900, 1915), as well as in the numerous intervening cognitive and contextual variables that influence memory reconstruction (Loftus and Hoffman 1989, Loftus and Klinger 1992), might reconstruction in a second language impact *further* on experiential recall, and, to our interests here—on the therapeutic working-through of conflictual and traumatic material? Integrating both clinical experience and research findings, Javier (1996) posits that, notwithstanding the potential impact of repressive determinants, aspects of early experience may in fact be inaccessible to coordinate bilinguals who undergo treatment conducted in their second language.

PROJECTIVE TESTING EVIDENCE

Adding further to our actively evolving picture of the bilingual mind is information rendered from psychological projective testing of personality traits. These findings offer provocative evidence for language-associated differences in personality functioning. When bilinguals are administered projective tests under controlled conditions, they have been reported to manifest different character traits (Findling 1969), and display different types of ideational and emotional material depending on which language they are being tested in (Ervin 1964). Ervin found, in her administration of the Thematic Apperception Test to French-English speakers, that the projection of manifest character and the expression of affective content were influenced by the language of the report. The author queried whether a bilingual's languages could be associated with particular ways of being. She wisely noted the inextricable link between language and cultural behavior, and concluded her report with an open question: Did her bilingual subjects' seeming "dual personality" simply reflect a case of biculturalism, where a specific social or linguistic context simply cues a shift in conditioned social behavior? Or does language in fact provide a much more mutative and pervasive function which organizes, stores, and internally insulates sets of cognitive and affective experiences?

INTERPRETING THE FINDINGS

The reports offered here from multiple investigative perspectives begin to shape a fascinating picture. At the very least they suggest that each of the bilingual's languages may somehow function as an organizational schema for the storage and processing of experience. These schema seem implicated at the level of neural representation, conceptual organization, memory storage, and some manifest personality traits. In Chapter 5, it will be further proposed that a language code may also provide organizational properties for the processing of self experiences.

At this junction, however, the argument for the presence of a separation in the bilingual's language systems must also be given a balanced perspective. For example, bilinguals (and multilinguals) are well aware that there exist common denotive meanings for objects' and activities that cut across the idiosyncratic specifics ascribed by cultural meaning (Hakuta 1986). A *ball* in most parts of the world conjures a round spherical object; *walking* conjures the activity of traversing distance. Also, one cannot dismiss the physical research evidence for areas of dual-language representation in the cortex delineated by neurological experiments and implied by multiple bilingual aphasia studies. At the experiential level, of course, those of us who are bilingual know that we *can* manage to recount an event in a language other than the language of the experience, as well as switch languages mid-sentence while expressing the same idea.

In fact, the notion of strict bifurcation between compound and coordinate bilinguals is no longer popularly maintained by linguists, who now espouse the notion of partially compound and partially coordinate systems in all bilinguals (Albert and Obler 1978). This is to say that there probably exists a significant degree of dynamic interdependence between the bilingual's language systems, for learning a new language, at whatever the person's age or context, still builds on some basic principals of linguistic universals developed at the time of the initial language acquisition, such as, for example; the child's use of multisensorial cues to ascribe meanings to words (Bucci 1994), or the basic operations that transform underlying conceptual meaning to surface phonological realization (Albert and Obler 1978). In addition, many languages share common phonemes, cognate words, and grammatical structures and rules, while also carrying their own idiosyncratic meanings and structural rules. It is therefore unlikely that a bilingual individual could be labeled entirely compound or entirely coordinate, or that a bilingual's language systems are either entirely interdependent or entirely independent from each other. Even the most recent neural localization work by Kim and colleagues (1997) showed not only cortical structures that were commonly activated by general language use, but also cortical structures that were activated by specific use of each of the coordinate bilingual's respective languages.

I believe that the questions pertinent to clinicians' interests are not whether and to what degree languages are independent or interdependent, but how and under what circumstances the languages of the bilingual do interact. We have already traversed an abundance of evidence that poses some level of duality and interaction in the bilingual's language systems. However, what we clinicians need to ask is whether there are any *psychodynamic* processes which create valences toward particular language choices. Posed differently, are there any psychodynamic processes involved in the relative interaction of language systems? In my view, this is the operational interface of bilingual language functioning that can be illuminated by psychodevelopmental and psychoanalytic principles of mental operation.

From his extensive work in bilingual phenomena, Paradis (1980a,b) developed a hypothesis that was intended to account for the presence of both coordinate and compound bilingualism in all dual-language speakers. His view, however, is also extremely compatible with the integration of psychodevelopmental and psychoanalytic phenomena. Paradis proposed that bilinguals possess a common conceptual store for the mental representations of experiences, events, things, and so on, and that there also exists a separate store of specialized, idiosyncratic meaning tags which each language (as an expression of its culture) has ascribed to the basic conceptual meaning. I believe that it is in the interaction between Paradis' notion of a basic conceptual store (or representation) of an object or experience, and the idiosyncratic meaning it is given by a specific language culture that (1) internalized interpersonal interactions and (2) psychodynamic processes enter the linguistic arena as significant vectors in the production of language activity.

The previous chapter reviewed some aspects of the mutative influence of internalized primary social interactions on words, and the specialized idiosyncratic meanings that a small two-person society (i.e., parent–child dyad), or large ethnocultural society can ascribe to a word symbol. Chapter 4 will explore these operations from a psychodynamic and clinical perspective. It will discuss data that emerge from the psychodynamic treatment method, whose narrative productions are far more complex and multiply determined than the methodologies utilized by psycholinguistic and neurocognitive research.

The organizational picture of the bilingual mind that has been painted thus far is a complex one. It offers information from multiple perspectives and levels of operation, that indicates there exist some differences in the organizational schema which maintain the bilingual's respective language systems. There is evidence denoting these organizational separations at the cognitive, linguistic, and personality trait levels. These organizational systems, however, are neither mutually exclusive, entirely independent, nor characteristic of all bilinguals, for indications of separate linguistic systems are found mainly in those who have learned their languages separately. With these parameters in mind, we can now explore the bilingual person in the clinical setting, where we will find the most fascinating dimension of bilingual functioning: the dialectical interaction between dual-language use and psychodynamic processes.

4

The Psychodynamics
of Bilingualism

EARLY PSYCHOANALYTIC OBSERVATIONS

Reaching back into the beginnings of modern clinical treatment for psychological disorders, and the origins of the psychodynamic view of psychological processes (i.e., the view that both conscious and unconscious psychic processes move human action, experience, and thought) is the seminal work of Sigmund Freud. The polyglot world of Freud's patient population in turn-of-the-century Vienna was a subject pool rich in potential for studies on bilingualism in the context of the linguistic data that we possess today. Freud was a monolingual German speaker who conducted all of his professional work in that language. With his invention of the psychoanalytic method and the growth of his clinical reputation came requests for treatment from an international patient population, people who were not native German speakers but who possessed sufficient command of German to undergo therapy with him in that language. For example, Marie Bonaparte was a native French speaker (Gay 1988), and the Wolf Man (Obholzer 1982) was a native Russian; a host of English-speaking Americans also consulted with Freud (Menaker 1989).

These were analyses conducted in the patients' secondarily acquired German. I have often wondered about the course of these treatments, the information produced by their free associations, and whether these narratives would have been different had they been related by these patients in their native languages. Notwithstanding the anxiety, discomfort, and resistance

inherent in any patient who presents for treatment, one wonders how, in addition, these first psychoanalytic patients negotiated the communication of their symptoms in a language probably learned later in their lives and disconnected from their early
developmental experiences. How did this impact on the reporting of their phobias, obsessions, and ultimately their sexual and
murderous desires? Had these pivotal cases in Freud's development of psychoanalytic theory been able to present themselves
in the language of their primary psychosexual worlds, might the
psychic landscapes from which Freud generated his conceptual
ideas have contained different dimensions of information for
theoretical rendering? This is a fascinating question which is
beyond the scope of this book, but which certainly merits its own
comprehensive inquiry in the future.

In his complex metaphysical descriptions of unconscious
processes, Freud ascribed a particular function to words and
verbal speech. He viewed word presentations as the purview of
the Conscious (Cs.) system, and that which permitted entrée of
primitive impulses and object cathexes of the Unconscious (Ucs.)
realm into the Preconscious/Conscious (Pcs./Cs.) system (Freud
1915). However, it was not until 1949 and 1950 that publications
began to appear from other classical analysts proposing that treatment in a patient's second language (i.e., an alternate set of word
representations) might impact on the analytic process, because
it could leave certain important areas of the patient's intrapsychic
world unavailable to consciousness. In 1949, Edith Buxbaum, an
analyst trained in Vienna and practicing in the United States,
published a report of her treatments with four bilingual German-
English patients. Buxbaum was herself a native German speaker
who had learned English as an adult. Working from a classical
Freudian model, she stated that the treatments had given her
"occasion to observe the way in which the ego and superego contribute to the acquisition and use of a second language"
(Buxbaum 1949, p. 279). One of her cases was that of a woman
who had migrated to the United States from Germany as an adolescent. This patient expressed a great deal of anxiety and pre-

occupation about male sexuality. This symptom, however, showed little sign of movement in the therapy until the patient happened upon her German schoolgirl slang for sexual terms. Buxbaum described how these language-specific associations stimulated the release of repressed memories involving forbidden sexual feelings that the woman had experienced as a child. Buxbaum found a similar process in many of her bilingual patients. She argued that for bilinguals in the treatment process, speaking in their secondarily acquired language, in effect constituted avoiding the language of their key fantasies and memories. Paralleling observations that had been made previously by Ferenczi (1911) about the unique affective power of early childhood words, Buxbaum stated that "childhood memories come alive in analysis only when the verbal expressions of that period are used" (1949, p. 283).

The following year in a paper aptly titled "The Mother Tongue and the Mother," Ralph Greenson (1950) described the analytic treatment of another bilingual German-English woman. The treatment was initially conducted in English. However the patient, on discovering that the analyst was bilingual in the same languages, refused to speak in German, claiming that "I have the feeling that talking in German I shall have to remember something I wanted to forget" (p. 19). She was also afraid of saying obscene or sexual words in German, feeling that they are "much easier to say and cleaner in English" (p. 119). She was correct about this, for upon finally using her native German, she did enter her early childhood world—a world whose specific language also evoked its memories, smells, and excitements. Greenson surmised that these experiences had remained heretofore well-guarded from the woman's consciousness and veiled by her "living" in a second language system, a system which did not easily evoke these sensual associations from the past. Thinking along the psychodevelopmental lines of the Freudian metapsychology, Greenson proposed that, for this particular client, German was the preoedipal language, and the locus of her unresolved infantile needs. English, learned at a later developmental period, offered the patient a ready defense system for warding off early psychic structures, and helping her to repress feelings and attitudes associated with her early mothering. Greenson (1950) subsequently used the mother tongue as a clinical technique in the treatment—a way to break through the patient's defensive armature, so to speak, and make the early language-related material more accessible to the therapy work.

Contributing further to this new pool of clinical information on bilingualism and its role in the psyche was the consideration that language also possessed viable dynamic functions within the matrix of early psychodevelopmental experiences. Both the seminal psychoanalytic writers and many others who eventually followed them in the clinical literature emphasized the pivotal position of the mother tongue and its role as a distinctive feature (Loewald 1980) in the global experiences that comprise the mother–child matrix. The mother tongue was viewed as the container for the experiences of that developmental era (Buxbaum 1949, Greenberg 1991, Greenson 1950, Marcos and Alpert 1976, Marcos and Urcuyo 1979, Pérez Foster 1993a, 1996a). It held the fullest affective-cognitive complement of those experiences, and as a symbolic representation was closest to actual lived experience. Thus the use of this language in the treatment situation could potentially offer more facile entrée into the experiences of that era. On the other hand, such linguistic segues into unresolved or traumatic developmental territory could also prove extremely anxiety provoking.

In 1955, Eduardo Kraph, a psychoanalyst working in and reporting from Argentina, began to describe the various ways in which his polyglot psychotherapy patients used their multiple language abilities to fend off anxiety. He pointed out, as did other writers (Greenson 1950, Marcos et al. 1977, Rozensky and Gomez 1983), that the nonprimary object languages possessed a ready capacity for use in the isolation of affect and intellectualization of emotional material. Languages learned later in a person's life contained neither the audial resonances nor real connection to the primary object experiences of early development. In addition, the ego-psychological perspective of the time viewed later acquisition of new language as occurring through the operation of the conflict-free sphere of the ego (Thass-Thienemann 1973). These new languages would come to be associated with new, varied, and further developed general ego and coping functions. They therefore possessed the psychic ability and adaptive capacity to defensively split off anxiety-ridden components of internal fantasy and primitive mental life. Indeed the experience of enhanced emotional control in bilinguals when speaking in their second language has been subsequently reported by many clinicians (Javier 1989, Pérez Foster 1996a,c, Stern 1993). Interestingly, for the patients themselves, awareness of this experience is usually not very far from consciousness. Note, again, the insightful comment made by Greenson's (1950) patient: "I have the feeling that talking in German I shall have to remember something I want to forget" (p. 19).

The early observations made by Buxbaum (1949), Greenson (1950), and Kraph (1955) clearly carried important clinical implications for bilingual patients at many levels of technical, theoretical, psychodynamic, and psychodevelopmental consideration. With respect to clinical technique, they noted for the first time the important role that a language code plays in releasing unconscious material into the treatment process. Use of the early language in clinical session seemed to allow for the reconstruction of early nodal experiences and affects that did not occur while the second language was in use. The second language seemed to possess a defensive capacity, and in the treatment situation could function in the service of resistance. Thus language choice could operate in tandem with psychically determined repressive mechanisms, as a way of avoiding immersion into anxiety-provoking events experienced and coded in another language.

However, in light of the psycholinguistic phenomena reviewed in the previous chapter, might these clinicians have also in fact been observing the operational evidence for dual-language systems, or bilingual language independence, such that experience coded and processed in the language system of early life was not as easily accessible to complete reconstruction in a language system learned in a different environmental context? We note that Buxbaum (1949) and Greenson (1950) were working in the clinical situation with narratives far more elaborate than the word lists used in psycholinguistic methodologies. The psycholinguistic research used word association tasks to study the interaction of the bilingual's language systems. The clinicians, on the other hand, were in the position of observing some unique and very complex intervening variables in the determination of bilingual language usage and interaction: these were *psychodynamic processes*. Inadvertantly, Buxbaum (1949), Greenson (1950), and Kraph (1955) had framed the possibility for a fascinating dialectic between bilingual language interaction and psychodynamic mechanisms.

It was not until twenty-five years later, however, that Luis Marcos and his colleagues would integrate the psychodynamic aspects of bilingual functioning, observed by the early analysts, with psycholinguistic and neurolinguistic phenomena. Marcos was a Spanish psychoanalyst who trained and practiced in metropolitan New York, a city with a large Latin American immigrant population. Contributions by him and his co-authors (Marcos 1972, 1976, 1979, Marcos and Alpert 1976, Marcos and Urcuyo 1979, Marcos et al. 1973a,b, 1977) stated that, given the multidisciplinary research evidence suggesting a separation in language systems, especially those of the coordinate bilingual, the relative degree to which the systems interact, notwithstanding the operational psycholinguistic dynamics of dual-language acquisition, usage, interaction, and interference (Grosjean 1982, Vaid 1986), could also be determined by their psychic conflictual valence. An experience lived, communicated, processed, and coded in a particular language system, if anxiety-provoking or threatening to the psychic equilibrium, could remain inaccessible to memory through content-specific or global avoidance of communication in that language. These clinicians framed an even more complex and multivariate view of bilingual language interactions: now to be considered in the operation of the bilingual psyche were the potential interactions of dual-language usage, separations in linguistic systems, and the influence of psychically driven repressive mechanisms.

The implications for all of these propositions were clinically quite far-reaching. First, language use in the bilingual's psychic system had now been assigned psychodynamic properties. Language, already complexly seen as a container of lived experience (Lacan 1977), a titrator of desire (Freud 1915), a cultural template of reality (Sapir 1949), and a voice of self and other (Vygotsky 1962)—if indeed represented by two symbolic code systems—could also be viewed as dynamically involved in a myriad of creative anxiety-reducing and probably stability-enhancing psychic processes. Secondly, these propositions began to implicate language as a formidable intervening factor in the reconstruction and clinical treatment of early psychic trauma. It would follow that the language of assessment and clinical intervention would be key to the recovery process. I will turn full attention to these issues in Parts II and III of this book.

CONTEMPORARY PSYCHOANALYTIC PERSPECTIVES

In the reported literature, much of the direct clinical work, as well as the theoretical understanding of the psychodynamic role of bilingualism in the psyche, has been based on the metapsychological assumptions of classical Freudian instinct theory. As is fitting to those drive-related constructs, language activities and differential language use are viewed within the basic context of expressive facilitation and inhibition of conflict-laden instinctual wishes. However, the last decade or so of contemporary psychoanalytic theory development has seen the burgeoning of object relations metapsychologies which have emerged from the British and American contributions of Winnicott (1965), Fairbairn (1952), Klein (1932), Mitchell (1988), Greenberg (1991), and others.

Interestingly, the field of psycholinguistics has undergone its own, and rather parallel, conceptual development, focusing a brighter light on the interpersonal matrices within which language is acquired (Bruner 1977, Dore 1979, Nelson 1990). The intimate world of the interpersonal dyad, especially the dyadic world of child and primary other, offers a prime view from which to additionally understand the psychodynamic role of language within object-relational processes. My own work in bilingualism has focused on the dynamic operations of language in the internalization of object relations, and its mutative influence on self formation and expression.

I began clinical work with clients who were bilingual in Spanish and English in 1975, well before I had read any of the literature that I have presented here. As the daughter of Latin American immigrants, I was fairly balanced in my Spanish-English verbal language capacity, for I had learned both languages from infancy—a compound bilingual. As a beginning clinician at that time, my perspectives about language were dominated by two major influences in my life: I was in a bilingual analysis, and I was convinced of the power of language in psychic life. These views were especially underscored by the fact that I had had a previous treatment in English only, which though extremely constructive for me, had nevertheless managed (cleverly) to steer clear of depths and distinctions of experience which later became the absolute centerpoints of my Spanish narratives in the second treatment. I related my bilingual experiences this way in a recent publication:

> I was born in urban New York to parents who migrated to the U.S. from Cuba and the Dominican Republic in 1930s. Spanish and English were expressive, vivid, and equally used modes of communicating in our daily lives. My language life today, in both external talk with others and inner talk with myself, still shifts between idioms, as aspects of my thinking, speaking, dreaming, remembering, and exclaiming all constitute domains of usage for each language.
>
> Yet I know—and I don't think that I am alone in this experience—that I have a deep transference to each of the idioms I speak. Each language for me is deeply symbolic of my relationships to my primary language teachers and the per-

sonal, environmental, and cultural meanings they ascribed to each tongue. Each language represents the intimate rules, implicit and explicit, that my caretakers established for being with them. This is true for the language of all individuals, whether mono- or multilingual; but for the child of a bilingual home, these rules also include what language to use when, with whom, and about what subject. Thus in the world of relationships within my family, each language included instructions about what part of me I could express, articulate, and develop through its use within a particular relationship. I used Spanish for loving my father, English for anger with my mother, Spanish for political discourse with everyone, and English for witty sarcasm with my aunts. These were rules about domains of language usage and experience in my home that were finer than the gross distinctions of Spanish for home and English for school, or Spanish for early trauma and English for defense. These were language instructions about how to express myself in the context of particular relationships which discoursed about particular things in a particular language. An outsider entering our home, listening to us on the global surface, could hear the facile manner in which we interchanged and switched from one language to another. They could not detect, however, the rules beneath the verbal surface—the world of meaning that the society of my family had ascribed to each idiom.

These language rules about self-expression within particular relational and environmental contexts became habits for me in language-related ways of functioning and, I would also say, "being." Although I have lived these language habits all of my life, they did not become clear and conscious to me until my own bilingual analysis. I came to understand that language modes of organizing my self expressions carried strong operational valences as I matured and began to discourse independently with the outside world. [Pérez Foster 1996b, pp. 142–143]*

* This segment first appeared in *Psychoanalytic Dialogues,* vol. 6, pp. 141–150, copyright © 1996 by Analytic Press, and is reprinted by permission.

Equipped with these very subjective language experiences, I was willing to enter the fray of my own patients' dual-language worlds. I used Spanish and English alternately, wherever patients led me: sometimes to penetrate experience, sometimes to skim it, but always to glean new understanding of inner worlds that had been organized by two different types of culturally embedded language symbols.

As I later became conversant in the literature of clinical bilingualism I was satisfied to find that many of my experiences were fairly consistent with those reported by other clinicians. I was particularly influenced by the body of work produced by Marcos and his colleagues. However, the release of more experience-near, affect-laden early information was not all I observed when the patient spoke his or her native tongue or switched from English to the native language in session. I observed another much more powerful and emotionally palpable phenomenon: this was that the transference and its ensuing countertransferential complement often switched as well. I emphasize the vibrancy of this phenomenon because it took place live, in the here-and-now of the intersubjective space between the patient and myself. As the patient shifted the language of his or her narrative for an extended period of time, so did they seem to shift the specific aspect or facet of the self that was speaking, and the object (vis-à-vis the therapist) that was being spoken to. My signal that this had taken place was not only the music of the new language, but often my own transformation in the presence of the patient who, through language, could sculpt me into another. This is to say that immersion in the patients' new language space probably rendered me more accessible to identification with the patients' projections, because it created fresh points of intersubjective contact on new sensorial and symbolic levels.

I posited (Pérez Foster 1992) that it was not only the developmental accuracy of speaking in the mother tongue which rendered early intrapsychic experiences more available in a treatment, but also the unique accessibility of the therapist who,

through speaking in the patients' early language, offered enhanced transformational possibilities for both transference enactments and projective identifications. Moving in dialectical process with this intersubjective/interpersonal phenomenon is use
of the linguistic symbol system in which certain formative developmental experiences take place, and which psycholinguistic
research has suggested will render the fullest memory reconstruction and recall (Javier et al. 1993, Laren 1997). I originally illus-
trated these observations with the following case example:

The Case of Anna

A 20-year-old Chilean dance student was recently referred to
me by her physician after a rapid 20-pound weight loss, for
which he found no organic etiology. Anna is a scholarship
student with a large dance company in New York City who
migrated to the U.S. to pursue dance professionally. She has
been in New York for 8 months and reports depressed mood
and loss of appetite. Anna spends her days in constant movement—rehearsing, taking classes, and babysitting for extra
money. This is her first time away from home. Anna weighs
85 pounds. She is fluid and birdlike in her movements, but
her voice, social manner, and habit of looking one straight
in the eye command undivided attention. At our first meeting, Anna admits that her "nerves" are the cause of her
weight loss. She is either too busy or nervous to eat. Though
Spanish is clearly her first language, Anna states that she
wishes to conduct her sessions in English in order to improve
her language proficiency. I do not comment on this as it is
my custom to follow the patient's lead with the language
spoken in session, but make note that Anna has chosen to
see a Spanish-speaking therapist, has been referred by her
own South American physician, yet will not speak in her
native tongue! Anna fills the hour with perfectly enunciated
English, describing her daily difficulties and her struggles to
compete for the dance scholarship. She speaks of her early
years sparingly—only when asked. Anna reports that our
sessions are helpful. She appears brighter, a little heartier,

and has even gained a few pounds. I am puzzled by this after 1½ months of visits; I feel I know nothing of this young woman's inner life, other than that she wants to be a ballerina and perfect her English! On a day when I am feeling particularly frustrated with her, she gets up to leave and drops her wallet with all of its contents. Coins roll on the carpet. I exclaim spontaneously in Spanish, "Oh dear, you've dropped your change!" (¡Ay, se te ha caido el dinero!) She mumbles "Sí," then looks at me with a mixture of surprise and fear. She looks as if she has seen a ghost! This girl with the fluid movements and perfect manners awkwardly gathers her change and leaves without even a farewell glance. Something has clearly happened between us. Anna calls to cancel two sessions in succession—she is sick with flu.

Not only am I impressed by Anna's behavior, but I am stunned by my own reaction to these events. Indeed, something has happened between us and I have committed the blunder. What came over me to comment on her change in Spanish and not follow my own rule to let patients take the language lead? I have frightened her, scared her away—too much too soon—I have even made her sick!

Anna returns in a mood that is colder and more reserved than usual. She spontaneously comments that she wonders whether I have her best interests in mind, as my speaking to her in Spanish shows that I must not want her to succeed in this country or practice her English conversation. She is clearly furious with me for my comment. I now begin to understand the power behind my own countertransferential experience. Anna had placed it in me the moment she looked at me in fear; she had transformed me into a powerful and threatening object (Bollas 1987).

In the ensuing sessions, she cries for the first time, expressing how lonely and homesick she is and how she fears that "turning into skin and bones" is proof that she does not know how to take care of herself. The only way she has been able to survive the 8 months in this country is to be tough, to not speak Spanish except when her family calls and to become "dura como un gringo" (tough like a cold-hearted American). She will not speak Spanish. My comment, she says, reminded her of the life she left behind. As she rails against her native tongue she also begins to speak. I subsequently find out that the proud mother who speaks of her socially as her "bailarina Americana" had begged her not to leave home, had implied that she herself might die if left alone, and had always intrusively and tenaciously possessed Anna as a narcissistic extension of herself.

Anna seems to tell us that speaking in her native tongue would force her to reenact with me an aspect of herself that she is trying desperately to deny. In English, her second language, she is strong, brave, and independent. In Spanish she is her mother's frightened, dependent child. My supposedly spontaneous exclamation in Spanish was in effect an interpretation, albeit unconscious, something like "let's move along with this—you are hiding behind your English—you have so many other feelings inside."

My point here is that not only did the introduction of the native tongue help to affectively stimulate important intrapsychic material relating to separation issues, but it did so through a transference enactment that might not have as readily taken place had the treatment proceeded solely in the second language.

Anna's case provides a graphic example of the powerful explosion of early developmental material that can occur in switching to the native tongue in treatment. It is also illustrative of early observations made from a classical psychoanalytic viewpoint, that living in a second language can function as a defensive armature against early developmental conflicts, isolating or splitting off old psychic structures from newer ones (Buxbaum 1949, Greenson 1950, Kraph 1955). Marcos and Alpert (1976) suggested that the bilingual individual may operate with a dual sense of self, with each language linked to different object relations, ego defenses, as well as distinct ego ideals. This thinking would certainly apply to the case at hand. The patient, Anna, clearly tells us of the vulnerable, birdlike self who belongs to mother and the Spanish-speaking world, and of the emotionally hardened, driven, ambitious American ballerina who is her self ideal. [Pérez Foster 1992, pp. 69–71]*

BILINGUALISM AND OBJECT RELATIONS

As a contemporary psychoanalytic clinician, however, I also integrated viewpoints from object relations theories, infant developmental research, and the intersubjective perspective of transference–countertransference. This latter view of the transference phenomenon views it as a joint creation of therapist and client, emerging from the multiple levels of their mutual interaction. I came to view "treatment in the native tongue [as] uniquely evocative of the self and object world in its native developmental environment" (Pérez Foster 1992, p. 71). Shifting to the developmental language seems to set the interactional stage, create a sensorial mood, trigger language-specific associations and more easily move client and therapist into self and object reenactments of that early developmental period.

In discussing aspects of language in the analytic process, Mitchell (1991) recently described language as the potential evoker of "original feeling states and earlier versions of self in relation to significant others" (p. 144). I would add to this that the power of language and the word to evoke early relational environments does not lie only in the evocation of original feeling states. For the patient who has regressed in treatment to an early verbal level, the "word" also evokes the original meaning as it was understood within the intersubjective operations of the child's primary object dyad. Using the lingual words of that dyad evokes the meaning system created within its intersubjective operations. In Chapter 3 of this book, Vygotsky's view of the acquisition of word meanings as a dynamic interpersonal and in-

---

*This segment first appeared in *Psychoanalytic Psychology,* vol. 9, pp. 61–76, copyright © 1992 by Lawrence Erlbaum Associates, and is reprinted by permission.

teractive process between caretaker and child was discussed
(1988, 1962). He views all speech as originating for the primary
purpose of interpersonal communication. Language originally
develops in the service of mother and child being with each
other. The meanings ascribed to words, the link between lingual
code and a real event in the world, is something that parent and
child, then sibling and child, friend and child, teacher and child,
and so on, negotiate in the context of their mutual and shared
experiences. For Vygotsky, interpersonal discourses in the context of these relationships become internalized as intramental
representations. This view of language acquisition places the
process at the very core of object relations, and underscores the
pivotal role of intersubjective relatedness between child and other
in the language acquisition process.

The relevance and application of Vygotsky's original views
to psychodynamic clinical treatments is quite clear, stated Wilson and Weinstein (1990): the unique word meanings of early
object relations "can only be brought into awareness within the
concept of transference—as the transference recreates some aspects of the earlier relationships and the defenses mobilized
during the act of word acquisition" (p. 35). I would add that
these unique word meanings clearly lie within the original lingual codes, and that the full complement of their cognitive, affective, and intersubjective meanings will be optimally understood
within the transference that utilizes that original code. As patient
and therapist struggle to understand each other, to work through
defenses, and to define and articulate the patient's particular
internal state of the moment, they are in fact reenacting the
intersubjective operations of the child and important other who
long ago negotiated a consensual word meaning for and understanding of that very self-state. Language and object relations are
inextricably linked in the psychic developmental process. And the
myriad associations, idiosyncratic meanings, and affective components of early language, as they came to represent early developmental experience, are probably optimally accessed in their
original language form. Thus for children who are raised in a

bilingual home, or who simultaneously learn another language in a separate context (e.g., English in school—Haitian Creole at home), language will become deeply linked to the relationships, contexts, and experience of self "lived" during the acquisition of those codes. Adding to the rich relational complexity of these bilingual experiences is that each of these languages will contain its own cultural template for organizing and shaping experience, as well as carry its own contextual rules about what language to use when, with whom, and for what topic.

5

The Bilingual Self

At some point in my clinical work and theoretical considerations, I turned my attention to the early self, and wondered more specifically about its connection to the dual language process. Impressed by clients in treatment who labored to integrate often disparate elements of their bicultural and bilingual lives, and keenly aware of the role of language in the organization of experience, I began to explore the dynamic function of language as a "characterological organizer." The works of Edgcumbe (1981), Harris (1992), and others in the area of developmental psycholinguistics had begun to describe the development of language in the child as an important site for self construction and the evolution of self identity.

In several papers (Pérez Foster 1993a, 1994, 1996a,b,c) I attempted to shape the notion of what I called a "bilingual self." I proposed that bilinguals may possess different experiences of the self that are organized by their respective languages. It was my thesis that each language is unique in evoking the relational experiences and social-contextual environment at the time of its original acquisition and early usage. *Condensed* within each language are both the verbal symbols and the important other who offered those symbols. *Alive* within each symbol are its semantic meaning and the interiorized versions of the self and that other who mutually shared and negotiated common experiences and gave them a name.

Contemporary psychoanalytic viewpoints posit that it is out of early experiences with others that aspects of the self are constructed (Klein 1932, Fairbairn 1958, Guntrip 1968, Kohut 1971). Mitchell (1991) adds that varied interactions with another embody active patterns of experience and behavior organized around a particular point of view, a way of being, and a sense of oneself. For the multilingual person, I believe that early object relations and the specific language they were negotiated in are critically yoked and intertwined and, as such, interiorized within the complex and variegated matrix of self representations. Internally, each language codifies or symbolizes the self with other. In the world of lived experience, each language evokes that self construction with the other in all of its affective, cognitive, behavioral, and imagistic elements, carrying with it the dynamic parameters of self-expression and inhibition established by the internalized object relation. I saw a reasonable connection between the hypothesis of a language-related self representation and the wide range of research offering compelling evidence for language-related differences in cortical organization, information processing, and manifest ego functioning.

The presence of organizational structures, which maintain some separation in dual-language systems, is not inconsistent with the notion of psychostructural organization of self experience that is language-related as well (Pérez Foster 1996a). Influenced by Hakuta's perspectives on bilingualism (1986), I viewed the bilingual person as a packaging puzzle, as it were, in which two "language-bounded experiential systems are housed in the confines of a single mind. It is as if their internal life and experience of self comprise a delicate duet of voices emanating from two different symbolic worlds that must coexist, cooperate, and probably compete to ultimately form the illusion of a harmonized self" (Pérez Foster 1996a, p. 101).

Essentially, the idea that the human psyche possesses a number of self representations which have been internalized from repetitive self-state experiences with various primary relationships is not a novel one. The current era in contemporary psychoanalytic theory-building has generated new dynamic formulations on the organization of the psyche that posit the presence of a variety of internalized self organizations that are deeply grounded within the psychic structure and possess unique defensive positions, ego operations, and coping mechanisms (Bromberg 1993, 1996, Davies 1996). The notion of multiplicity in self organization, garnered from the recent focus on dissociative disorders in trauma victims, sheds light on the general range of patients that we see in our consulting rooms, whose deep disavowal of or dissociation from specific segments of their self experience seem far too circumscribed and context-specific to be explained simply by the operation of pan-repressive mechanisms favored in earlier theoretical eras (Freud 1900). We have, I think, become much more refined in our psychodynamic understanding, and better educated in the power of the internalized object-relational matrix, which not only contains the image of the other but also the image of the particular self with that other, with all of its ensuing desires, conflicts, and psychic methods for dealing with them. The recent literature describes the psychic context that can maintain a particular internalized self representation in the depths of disavowal: its highly conflictual valence and perceived threat to the integrity and balance of the general psychic organization (Bromberg 1993, 1996).

As it is in the dynamics that operate in any deeply dissociated segment of the psyche, it is anxiety from conflict that creates and maintains a bilingual self-organization—schemas of language-bound self-representations that remain split off and unable to function as interdependent (and integrally functioning) parts of the whole character. Thus, given the conflictual valence of formative self-experiences that may have been lived and coded in a particular language, and the neurocognitive valence, if you will, for organizational separations in linguistic systems, there exist, in my view, strong influences toward the creation of self organizations that are both bounded by and dissociated through language.

The Case of Yulie

The following is a case I initially published to illustrate these dynamics. It is the case of a bilingual Spanish-English speaking woman whom I saw in treatment for five years. The most intriguing aspect of her therapeutic process was a progressive unfolding of two highly conflictual self-schema that appeared to be organized or encapsulated by the patient's respective languages. Each of these schema seemed to have its own, well-articulated psychic identifications, defensive structures, and functional ego operations.

> The patient, a 40-year-old Cuban mother of two, sought consultation with me for depression and verbal outbursts of rage toward her children. Yulie has been married for 15 years to an extremely successful Cuban corporate lawyer who is in private practice with two partners. Yulie and her husband are urban, socially ambitious, and active in local politics. She is extremely proud of her position on the community board of her district, a post for which she actively campaigned. She is her husband's office manager. She handles all billings, manages support staff, has designed a new suite of offices for the practice, and just transferred all office business onto a computer software system that she taught herself to operate. The patient has a high school equivalency diploma.
>
> Yulie migrated to this country at age 6, at the time of the Castro revolution. In Cuba, her father was an engineer and her mother a schoolteacher. Both parents bitterly opposed the communist occupation in their country and vowed never to return until Castro was overthrown. Yulie describes her parents during the early years in the U.S. as consumed with politics and the bitter downgrading of their socio-economic status. Indeed, Yulie's father, portrayed as an opinionated and fearless man, took part in the abortive Bay of Pigs invasion in 1961, in which he died. Yulie speaks of her father in heroic terms, "Papi left us, but he died for Cuba."
>
> At our first meeting, the patient is gracious and poised despite her nervousness. She is groomed in a distinctly American tailored style, but her social manner is rather courtly in an old-fashioned, Caribbean sort of way that is familiar to me. She calls me *doctora*, mentions that I have been well rec-

ommended, asks permission to be seated, and states that we Latins should get along well. Our conversation to this point has all been in Spanish, including the initial phone contact. I deliberately followed Yulie's language lead, as is my custom with bilingual patients. Thus in Spanish she willingly shares the unhappiness of her present marriage. Her husband is domineering and demeaning and never fails in an argument to remind her of her inferior education. In her frustration, she has been exploding at the children and seeks therapy to *controlar mis rabias* (control my rages).

Yulie struggles to compose herself. Now about 20 minutes into this first session, the patient asks if she can continue the session in English. She says, "It is just that in English I can express myself so much better. I know exactly what I want to say. English is my strong language because I went to school here." It's okay, I say, then at a later point ask her, "In what language do you live with your husband?" She says, "Oh, in Spanish only." I begin to wonder here what role Yulie's language may play in her sense of self and her relational mode with others.

Yulie begins to see me twice weekly. She continues to speak only English. In the ensuing months she talks of the tumultuous and chaotic adolescent years after her father's death:

"My mother cried all the time, never slept, and lost 60 pounds. She heard my father's voice. She hardly took care of us. This went on for years. I was no angel when I got older. I gave my mother a lot of grief. I went out with one boy after another. She called me a tramp. We were killing each other. She would lock me out of the house. Finally I ran away with my boyfriend at 16. But it didn't work out after a year. My mother wouldn't let me come back home—she said I was no good. I lived with my aunt, got my act together, started getting good jobs—then I met Orlando. My mother couldn't believe that an educated man would want to marry me. She tells me to put up and shut up with him. After all, he's my only hope to be a decent person. I should remember how lucky I am that he married me."

Approximately six months after beginning treatment, Yulie brings in a dream:

She is in the playground with her children. Other mothers are sitting on park benches. They are talking and their voices get louder, and now the women are turning into *cocatúas*. She uses this Spanish word for a type of Caribbean parrot. I ask her in what language she had the dream. "I always dream in Spanish," she says. I ask her to continue telling me the dream in this language.

"*Las mujeres se vuelven cacatúas. Es increible. Empiezan a volar alrededor de mi. No se callan. Quieren que yo no hable. Estan gritando; pájaros feos. Corro pero no las puedo escapar. Yo me despierto en una pesadilla con pánico.*" [The women are turning into *cocatúas*. It's incredible. They start to fly toward me. They don't quiet down. They don't want me to say anything. They are screaming—the ugly birds. I run away, but can't escape them. I wake up in a nightmare, in a panic.]

In the following sessions, Yulie continues to talk of the dream and its associations to her mother. For the first time since the initial twenty minutes of our first meeting, she uses Spanish in session, at times alternating with English, but now seemingly drawn to speaking her native language as she begins painfully to recount her mother's verbal abuse and abandonment.

I also notice something else happening at this juncture. Yulie begins to assume a much more comfortable, settled-in position with me. Around this time she switches from the formal *usted* to the more familiar *tú* in addressing me. I see this as a sign—of something. The language has drawn us closer—possibly. But then she begins to be late for sessions. First a few minutes, then up to fifteen minutes. She is breezy about this, at times not even explaining. I find myself annoyed at her attitude. On another occasion she has her receptionist call to cancel her session. I am starting to steam. On another occasion she brings two friends, who sit and wait outside during the session. I grumble to myself, "What is this, a public waiting room?" Finally one day she pays my bill (late) with a crumpled check dug out of the bottom of her bag. Is this a shabby check for shabby service? I'm really steaming now!

The countertransferential process has become palpably clear. Subjectively I have become an unwitting partner in Yulie's very personal drama. She has successfully transformed me into a hacking Caribbean bird who wants nothing more than to squawk at her, keep her in line, and make her behave. My first attempts to interpret this transference are met with anger and accusations. "You are just like everyone else trying to tell me what to do. You just sit there and don't say much, then when you do, it is to criticize me. What are you doing in this kind of work anyway—Latin women can usually never keep their mouths shut!" (I believe that Yulie is pointedly interpreting here a dimension of my own bilingual self split).[1] The mother tongue has indeed transformed us both!

Yulie is fighting and working. It is tough going. We live almost entirely in Spanish now. She speaks in English, seemingly to rest, and I must say that I feel relief at these times. In the months and years to come we get to know that mother's grief and agitated depression were probably of psychotic proportions and that she harbored jealous resentment that Yulie had been the light of her father's eyes.

As we began to reconstruct, Yulie's development in the English-speaking American world served a dual function. After her father's death when she was 12 years old, she had im-

---

1. An unexplored aspect of bilingual psychoanalysis is the analyst's clinical language-related self-experience. A recent paper by M. Stern (1993) points to changes in both the analyst's mood and in analytic technique upon shifting to their own native language in the treatment. This observation carries significant import, for it suggests the potential for tremendous variegation and complexity in transference–countertransference phenomena, all of which can become active material for the analytic work. See the section on Clinical Supervision in Chapter 10 for further discussion of this topic.

mersed herself in all things American with a vengeance: absolutely perfecting her English, excelling in school, and allowing herself to be "adopted" (as she called it) by several American teachers with whom she came to identify strongly. Thus, on one hand, the English code became developmentally the second symbolic medium through which she conducted particular relational experiences and came to evolve complex, creative, and adaptive functions in her self-development. On the other hand, English allowed her to ward off and efficiently encapsulate—as might any well-articulated characterological defense—the anguish of her early psychic life. This was the life and trauma with primary objects that she had internally organized in a different language: the actual loss of her father and the psychic loss of her mother and motherland. At the most deeply felt moments of "living" in her Spanish world in the treatment, Yulie came to reexperience herself as the girl child who had been punished and banished by mother for the oedipal crime of adoring her father. Yulie's heroic Americanized adage, "Papi left us, but he died for Cuba," simply became the mournful, *"Papa se me fué"* (Daddy left me). Linguistically, to be noted here is Yulie's use of the reflexive form of the verb "go" in Spanish, a form that does not exist in English syntax. It connotes that the verb has had a uniquely intimate and personal impact on the subject (the self) in the sentence (something like, Daddy has gone on me).

Yulie would also come to understand that at the core of her manifest marital difficulties was a torturous and complex dual transference to her husband as both idealized paternal figure and castigating envious mother. It was these two self-object configurations, these modes of being with another, that were so deeply symbolized in her Spanish, so cleverly guarded by her English, and so dramatically revived in the "theater" (McDougall 1989) of her bilingual analysis. [Pérez Foster 1996a, pp. 110–113]*

---

*This segment first appeared in *Psychoanalytic Dialogues,* vol. 6, pp. 99–122, copyright © 1996 by Analytic Press, and is reprinted by permission.

INTERPRETING THE PROCESS OF
BILINGUAL TREATMENT

In this case, the client's use of her native language in the clinical treatment undoubtedly released richer and more affect-laden material. This was the language of her primary object world. This finding certainly corroborates the observations of other clinicians who have reported on dual language use in the clinical setting (Buxbaum 1949, Greenson 1950, Kraph 1955). However, I observed in addition that the client's spontaneous language-switching in the treatment was also accompanied by a concurrent shift in the transference–countertransference paradigm (Pérez Foster 1992, 1993a, 1994, 1996a,c). As the client shifted the linguistic aspect of her clinical narrative, so did she seem to shift the specific aspect of the self that was speaking and the object (vis-à-vis the therapist) that was being spoken to. My cue that this had taken place was both the music, mood, and special meanings of her new language, as well as my own subjective transformation upon entering the patient's "Spanish language space." Our intersubjective communications had shifted to very different speaking terms.

In conducting bilingual treatments over the years, I have come to understand this process of what I call "lingual transference shifting" as occurring at varying levels of experience and psychic complexity. Starting at a basic experiential level of affect attunement and contagion (Emde et al. 1978, Klinnert et al. 1983, Stern 1985, Tronick and Adamson 1979), both members of the therapeutic couple are pulled into a sensorial space, an altered mood state some might say, which is evoked by the simple sensual prosody of the new language presence in the room. This experience is similar to the child and early caretaker's sharing of affective states and moods, which occurs prior to the sharing of mental states in the symbolic period (Stern 1985, Trevarthan and Hubley 1978). The physical and sensual experience of the new language probably also stimulates arousal of what Bucci (1997) would call sensorial or perceptual channels of the memory system; these are the sensorial dimensions of experience stored in memory. However, proceeding then to a more symbolic level, the new language usage in the treatment begins to signify new feeling states and cognitive experiences particular to the psychodevelopmental time of original language usage. As the new symbol system both expands and deepens in the work, so do the mood and signification shifts likewise expand within the relational dimension of the dyad. I believe that these multifaceted levels of new intersubjective contact stimulate both perceptual and symbolic language-associated memory. They arouse language-specific experience and evoke internalized self–other representations; ultimately culminating in robust transference phenomena.

Thus, condensed within each of the client's languages are both the verbal symbols and object relations, with accompanying self-schema, within which those symbols were learned. Working within these new verbal symbols in the treatment will yield fresh descriptive and semantic meanings. Additionally, it will stimulate the transferential enactment of the related interiorized versions of the self and primary other, who once mutually negotiated common experiences, and in the context of their relationship (and the language culture at large) gave them symbolic word meanings. I see these dynamic clinical phenomena as taking place in both compound and coordinate bilinguals. But I also hold that, for coordinate bilinguals who have learned their two languages in separate developmental contexts—and who may thus possess some degree of linguistic organizational separation (Kim et al. 1997)—access to the full complement of variegated affects, cognitions, and symbolisms contained within internalized experience will be more difficult to achieve in an alternate language.

LANGUAGE AS CHARACTEROLOGICAL ORGANIZER

In this section I have been trying to shape the idea that internalized representations of the self that arise from early object-relational experiences are deeply symbolized in the language system in which the object relations were actually lived. I have proposed that "the myriad impulsive, conflictual and ego-defensive elements associated with these self-states are represented within language-specific constellations of cognitive and affective meaning" (Pérez Foster 1996a, p. 115). If these language-bound self states are conflict-laden, and the opportunity is present for functioning in a different language, these conflictual states may remain dissociated from conscious availability, exerting a toll on the general psychic economy, and emerging through opportunistic lapses in the dissociative defensive structure, or through disavowed actions in transference enactment.

Seeking to argue this proposition beyond the domains of clinical setting or psychoanalytic theory, and to integrate it with the bilingualism literature from other domains, I have described similar analogues of language-specific organizational schema at neuro-representational and cognitive/information processing levels. Of particular note are the experimental findings of psycholinguistic researchers who note that coordinate bilinguals can often generate a separate series of idiosyncratic associations to the same word depending on what language it is presented in (Ervin and Osgood 1954, Kolers 1963, 1968). I view these operations as contributing to the organizational core of what might be considered a *language-bounded inner representation of the self* for many coordinate bilinguals. And the accessibility to this language-bound self is influenced both by psycholinguistic parameters (it cannot be fully accessed through an alternate language), and by psychodynamic mechanisms of a repressive or dissociative nature.

I am proposing that language, in its capacity to function as a symbolic representation of environmental and object-relational experiences, can serve as a self-schematic or characterological organizer for the bilingual. Language can come to signify particular patterns of psychological-behavioral self-states that occur together over time. This thinking is not inconsistent with the schematic model of memory organization that was pioneered by Bartlett (1932). In this model, the memory system, in order to accommodate the myriad volleys of incoming experiential stimuli, for the purpose of economy, organizes and schematizes experiences into categories, scripts, or prototypical units of knowledge (Bonnano 1990, Rosch 1978, Schank and Abelson 1977, Singer and Salovey 1988). More recently Stern (1985), Luborsky (1988), and Bucci (1997), have used similar schematic models to understand experiential self-states. As previous cognitive research with bilinguals has already shown language to function as an organizer of experience and subsequent recall in memory, it is reasonable to view a language code system as operating similarly, in the manner of a fairly comprehensive categorical synthesizer in the organization of affective, cognitive, behavioral, and object experiences associated with the self.

Bromberg (1993, personal communication 1994) has argued, however, that in the case of self-representations, other schematic organizers outside language could be posited just as validly. For example, affect has been proposed as the organizational foundation for the memory system, functioning as a broad categorical imperative for all other schematic processes (Tomkins 1962, 1981), with the affective tone surrounding self-related experiences playing a major role in both the perception, processing, and eventual categorization of the events. This thinking could certainly explain my patient Yulie's subjective transformation on entering the new mood of her "Spanish language space." What I have been viewing as a "lingual" transference shift based on linguistically organized self-states, might be cued by an affective mood shift, where it is a particular quality of language-related affective arousal that signifies or cues the change in self state.[2]

I would agree with this formulation, especially along the paradigmatic lines of early infant experience explored in the pre-

---

2. This phenomenon is similar to that reported in the multiple personality or dissociative identity disorder literatures, where the shift to an alter or dissociated personality state is sometimes cued by a specific state of affective arousal (Loewenstein and Ross 1992, Putnam 1984, 1988).

vious chapter, where the sensorial-affective sphere constitutes the primary organizational cornerstone of subjective experience and communication (Stern 1985, Tronick et al. 1979). This affective dimension of experiencing the world holds fast throughout development and remains as one of the basic experiential synthesizers. But we are also aware that as cognitive abilities begin to evolve in the infant, especially along the linguistic symbolic dimension, they assume new and extremely dynamic functions in the general processing and organization of external and subjective experience. "While I am not arguing for a linguistic imperative in the schematization of self-representational experience, I do want to underscore that language, by the very nature of its plastic, symbolic capacity and deep representational involvement in microrelational and macrocultural matrices, serves a powerful and highly mutative function" (Pérez Foster 1996a, p. 117).

The organizational role of language in both cognitive and psychodynamic processes has been a much overlooked phenomenon in clinical work with bilingual people. Reports from the American clinical literature selectively reviewed here, as well as a recent review of mainly European work on bilingualism by Amati-Kehler and colleagues (1993), underscore the key role of early language as the repository of early infantile experience. These reports also describe how language can be used by the polyglot in the service of psychic repression. In the treatment of bilingual speakers it is important to realize that their current language usage probably plays a dynamic role within their psychic lives, for language can mediate the conscious availability of internal and conflictual material, as well as the concordant dissociation from that material. I am further suggesting that the proficient speaker of two (or possibly more) languages may also possess *language-bounded inner representations of the self,* and that the relative independence or interaction of these self-organizations is similarly titrated by psychodynamic processes.

PART II

ASSESSING THE BILINGUAL PERSON

The multifaceted and multidisciplinary considerations that have been presented thus far have hopefully introduced the reader to the complex nature of the bilingual's living, developing, and experiencing in two language worlds. In Part II, we move forward into issues concerning the clinical assessment of the bilingual person, and explore the available fund of information that might guide the clinician in integrating some of the attendant factors that have been recognized as influencing the bilingual's psychic processes. The existent literature in this important area is frankly disappointing and still rather undeveloped, reflecting a lack of consciousness and academic/scientific attention to the needs of the hundreds of thousands of bilingual immigrant clients who seek our mental health services. I hope that this volume makes some contribution to the arousal of this consciousness, and am well aware that the guidelines offered in Parts II and III of this book are limited in the fund of data that informs them as of yet. But this is the exciting beginning of a new area of exploration, in which the face validity offered by clinical observations, the judicious integration of multidisciplinary literature, and the results garnered from single-subject or small N designs will hopefully translate into testable protocols and applications for the wider bilingual population.

In Chapter 6, "Clinical Diagnosis and Bilingualism," I place the problem of assessing bilingual people in the broader clinical context of cross-cultural assessment, and note some of the ethnicity-bound factors that influence diagnosis. In addition, I offer both quantitative and clinical literature that has emerged on the impact of bilingualism in symptom assessment and diagnosis. Two serious issues have impacted the investigations in this area: cultural bias in testing and assessment procedures, and the mixed pools of bilingual subjects that have been used in clinical studies. These latter subjects sometimes span a wide range of linguistic competence and have produced a confusing body of results that is difficult to decipher and integrate for the purpose of practical directives. I will make some attempt to do so.

In Chapter 7, "Taking a Psycholinguistic History," I propose the use of a guided inquiry format which is designed to access the psychodevelopmental and psychodynamic aspects of dual language ability. This assessment format is relevant to the psychodynamic treatment of bilinguals and can offer information on the role that dual languages play in character formation and symptom expression. The construction of this inquiry format was informed by much of the psychodevelopmental, psycholinguistic, and psychoanalytic literatures reviewed in Part I.

In Chapter 8, "Using Bilingual Translators," I explore and propose guidelines for what most cross-cultural clinicians consider a sad but necessary evil in the delivery of mental health services: the use of translators as aids in the evaluation of clients who have little or no command of the clinician's language. Unlike the private practitioner who can exercise options in patient selection, practitioners in overburdened agency and institutional settings often have no such luxury, as they can be presented with clients in acute distress and in need of evaluation in whose languages they are not conversant. The use of a translator in such situations constitutes a formidable set of challenges that spans issues of clinical accuracy, patient confidentiality, and therapeutic rapport. At this point in time no formal set of guidelines exists in the mental health profession for the use of these language aids, who can potentially exert an important influence on the course of a bilingual person's clinical disposition. I would like to offer a proposal for such guidelines, integrating interpreter criteria that have been established by the clinical field of communicative disorders (Gerver and Sinaiko 1978, Mikkelson 1983, Northcott 1984, Roe and Roe 1991, Stein et al. 1981). This field has developed a body of criteria for use by interpreters of American Sign Language, the official language of the deaf in the United States and Canada. These criteria include both technical and ethical guidelines for interpreters, and have recently integrated consideration of mental health contexts.

6

Clinical Diagnosis and Bilingualism

THE CULTURE/LANGUAGE INTERFACE
IN ASSESSMENT

The specific influences of language per se on clinical assessment, which are the particular concerns of this book, are in fact embedded within the broader matrix of cultural issues. The mental health field, at this point in its development, has come to understand that the complex needs of its clients need to be understood through the cultural milieus in which its clients function. Both clinicians and psychometric researchers have become increasingly aware of and alarmed about the inherent influences of both cultural and linguistic factors in the evaluation of human behavior. In addition, there is now a growing body of critical literature which roundly questions the universal application of Western perspectives on psychological function and dysfunction (Bruner 1986, Cirillo and Wapner 1986, Kirschner 1990).

In the domain of psychological testing there are the pervasive problems of testing bias, and the ethically questionable practice of using psychological instruments designed, standardized, and validated from American majority perspectives for the assessment of ethnic, linguistic, and socioeconomic minority groups (Malgady et al. 1987). While the controversies on these issues have mainly focused on intelligence testing and its impact on African-American subjects, there is now an emerging concern about the use of instruments which assess personality characteristics and psychopathological functions. These instruments are used with ethnic groups whose cultural and linguistic meaning systems may differ markedly from the American value criteria on which the measures have been constructed. Integrated within the administration procedures, factor construction, and parametric criteria of any diagnostic instrument are ethnocentric assumptions about what constitutes mental health and mental pathology. In the sphere of American-constructed diagnostic instruments that assess psychopathology, test items are often keyed to reflect pathology on an empirical basis, where items have been constructed and standardized from Anglo-American diagnostic samples (Guernaccia et al. 1996). The works of Padilla and Ruiz (1973), Malgady et al. (1987), and Guernaccia (1992, 1993) on the assessment of psychopathology in Hispanic subcultures, for example, conjointly point to the disturbing frequency with which many culturally syntonic behaviors, affects, and belief systems are erroneously diagnosed as pathological when assessed along the diagnostic criteria of Anglo-American functioning. Sue and Sue (1990) and others have found similar results when Asian groups are evaluated.

In an effort to grapple with and overcome what is erroneously believed to be simply a "language barrier" effect, and make assessment scales designed in English amenable for use by different ethnic populations, authors have sought to translate testing instruments into various other languages. An example of this, in the pressured and overcrowded school and agency systems of multiethnic urban centers, is the hasty and often unsystematic translation of instruments for administration to recently arrived immigrant children and adults. These translated instruments (if translated systematically) often demonstrate acceptable correlations with their English counterparts when administered to bilingual subjects; however, independent evidence of criteria-related validity with the separate ethnic groups has usually not been established. Simply put, a translated instrument becomes a new measure, one in need of its own validity, reliability testing, and standardization norms for the new group it is intending to assess. Furthermore, the question of content validity in the factor construction of American test products stands as a formidable scientific and epistemological problem when these products are used with non-American subjects. When administering our instruments to other ethnic groups, are we essentially testing for "American depression," "American intelligence," and "American psychosis"? The works of Yamagida and Marsella (1978), Lutz (1988), Jenkins (1994), and others, for example, note variations in culturally constructed meanings of numerous affective states, demonstrating noticeable differences in the factors that are mainstays of clinical diagnostic criteria for the Western affective disorders.

Adding further to the complexity of making clinical assessments in cross-cultural contexts, is the recognition in the literature of what are broadly termed "culture-bound syndromes" (Guernaccia 1993, LaBruzza and Mendez-Villarrubia 1994). These refer to coherent patterns of psychological distress manifested through affective, cognitive, and behavioral symptoms that are indigenous to certain cultural groups. These syndromes often overlap with *DSM-IV* categories, but seldom have a symptom-to-symptom relationship to *DSM-IV* diagnoses. In addition, Guernaccia (1992, 1993) notes, from his extensive work in this area, that culture-bound syndromes, unlike the criteria sets of *DSM-IV* diagnostic categories, do not view psychological symptoms as their only means of definition, but rather may also integrate the social, moral, or spiritual state of the person to identify a syndrome state.

The question of whether there exists a universal set of psychological symptoms which represent the same kind of distress in all people, or whether each cultural group contains its own array of syndromal expressions for distress within its milieu, is well beyond the scope of this book (Westermeyer 1987). However, I have presented the above discussion to alert the reader to the larger context of cultural differences in symptom expression, and the attendant difficulties in adequately assessing them.

CLINICAL ASSESSMENT AND BILINGUALISM

The issue of language, and its role as an expressor of distinct cultural meanings, is embedded within the complex matrix of potential cultural differences in the expression of psychological distress. In considering now how dual-language systems impact on the expression of symptoms and their subsequent assessment by the clinician, I would like to encourage the reader to bring to the fore the multidisciplinary information discussed in Part I on both the dynamics of speech in psychic processes, and the neurocognitive organization of language in the bilingual mind. These will provide helpful points of reference.

As succinctly stated by Oquendo (1994) in a recent report, "the evaluation of patients in a second language presents many pitfalls" (p. 616). This perspective is corroborated by many clinicians who report on their work with bilingual clients (Aragno and Schlachet 1996, Bradford and Muñoz 1993, Javier 1996, Pérez Foster 1996c). I view these pitfalls as subsumed within the following spheres of influence: (1) language impacting on symptom variance, and (2) second-language anxiety impacting on symptom variance.

Language and Symptom Variance

Probably one of the key concerns of any clinician who has referred to this volume is whether bilinguals can be adequately evaluated in their second language. In metropolitan urban centers, our concerns lie with the wide variety of ethnic patients who present for treatment. While the tides of ethnic representation in the mental health profession are very slowly changing to include diverse multiethnic clinicians in the ranks, the most common cross-cultural clinical situations are those of monolingual English-speaking clinicians evaluating ethnic patients who function at varying levels of English proficiency. Thus the question of whether anything other than the native language can render an accurate representation of the patient's mental life is key to us.

Research on how the language of the interview impacts on the assessment of severe psychopathology has yielded contradictory results. The findings confusingly denote both the native *and* second language, respectively, as the idioms in which patients manifest and/or express the most severe cognitive pathology. Del Castillo (1970), in what he admitted was an unsystematic approach, did a post hoc analysis of interviews administered over time to five bilingual psychiatric inpatients. He concluded that his patients appeared less psychotic when evaluated in English (their second language) than when interviewed in Spanish. Aware of his lack of experimental controls, he nevertheless conjectured that the patients' intellectual effort of expressing themselves in a foreign language stimulated the arousal of presumably higher-order defenses which were not present during the more regressed states of speaking in the mother tongue. Del Castillo contended that this helped maintain patients in better contact with reality, a position held by earlier writers such as Buxbaum (1949), Greenson (1950), and Thass-Thienemann (1973). The second language, acquired later in life, was thought to be associated with higher-level ego functions. The native language, on the other hand, recalled and aroused the regressive associations and primitive cognitive functions of the early infantile period. A case study reported by Laski and Taleporos (1977) similarly noted that the native language was the consistent venue utilized by a bilingual patient for their hallucinatory symptoms.

In a later study, Price and Cuellar (1981) replicated these earlier observations in a controlled design. Their Spanish-English schizophrenic patients also exhibited more psychopathology when assessed in their native language. In addition, the patients' verbal fluency and level of acculturation were found to be predictive of this language effect. This set of neatly corroborating findings is contradicted, however, by two 1973 reports published by Marcos and his colleagues (Marcos et al. 1973a,b). These authors found the exact opposite: that their controlled assessments of psychiatric inpatients manifested more psychopathology when patients were assessed in English, their second language. They reasoned, interestingly, that their patients, who were already experiencing subjective inner turmoil due to their condition, became even further disorganized with the pressure and effort of being assessed in English, their second language.

It is striking to note the dramatic discrepancy in the thinking used to explain such contradictory findings. Del Castillo (1970) had reasoned that his patients' use of their second language had provided binding functions against further cognitive disorganization. Marcos and his colleagues (Marcos et al. 1973a,b), on the other hand, viewed the demands of the second language as promoting more cognitive disorganization. Such contrasting findings raise a host of queries that will have to be answered by future exploration. However, clinicians are sufficiently alerted that the diagnostic assessment of any bilingual patient is no simple matter. Evaluation needs to proceed with caution, and with the probable necessity of a clinical assessment in each language, so that results can be compared and deliberated upon. The language–diagnosis conundrum, by the way, is even further deepened by the finding of Gonzales (1977) who observed *no* significant differences in the expression of psychopathology when bilingual inpatients were assessed in each of their respective languages.

Further research is abundantly indicated and it will need to integrate consideration of various methodologic, clinical, and dynamic factors. From the standpoint of methodology in psycholinguistic research, language proficiency in each language needs to be more carefully assessed, with a further distinction made between those bilinguals who learned their two languages in the same versus separate environmental or developmental contexts. This is a factor that has been heavily implicated in the psycholinguistic concept of language independence. A core clinical issue to be ultimately discerned, is the deep relationship between symbolic expression in language and cognitive organization. Are the noted manifest differences in level of cognitive organization and disorganization simply a function of verbal expression? Or are we observing manifest expression of true language-related differences in cognitive organization as such?

The heuristic and clinical fascination for those of us interested in bilingual processes is whether the supposed (neuro) cognitive separations, for those who have learned their languages in different environmental contexts, are also paralleled by differences in psychic and characterological functioning. The notion of a bilingual self has already been proposed based on the psycholinguistic concept of language independence, projective testing data on language differentials in personality characteristics, and psychodevelopmental factors (see Chapter 5). In addition, these proposed language-related self organizations are described as associated with distinct ego-defensive structures and ego coping and adaptive mechanisms (Greenson 1950, Marcos et al. 1977, Pérez Foster 1992, 1994, 1996a,b,c). The intriguing question for clinicians who are in the important position of assessing bilingual clients is: Would formal evaluation of each language-related self-state render a separate mental status, or different level or type of pathology?

We clearly have a long road ahead in the exploration of this area, with the need for well-designed methodologies (Vazquez 1982), and controls for linguistic proficiency, language acquisitional contexts, and diagnostic refinement. On this latter point, all research reported thus far on the bilingualism-psychotherapy interaction—and just reviewed above—was mostly done on hospitalized schizophrenics or symptomatically psychotic patients (Del Castillo 1970, Gonzales 1977, Laski and Taleporos 1977, Marcos et al. 1973a,b). Notwithstanding that more work needs to be done with diagnostic groups suffering with far lesser degrees of cognitive pathology, it should be noted that the studies with schizophrenic inpatients confounded both acute and chronic schizophrenic types as well as paranoid and nonparanoid dimensions. These are parameters in the schizophrenic spectrum that are well-established as manifesting significant differentials in cognitive processes, differentials that may have influenced assessed level of pathology in the bilingual studies (Herron 1977,

Magaro 1980). Del Castillo's subjects (1970) were longer-term hospitalized patients, whereas those studied by Marcos and colleagues (1973a,b) were recently hospitalized schizophrenics in an acute state of psychotic decompensation. In addition, no studies distinguished paranoid from nonparanoid types of schizophrenics in their subject pools, thus confusing a distinction that is marked by different patterns of cognitive symptom presentation (Neufeld 1977, Pérez Foster 1981, Ross and Magaro 1976). This was another source of symptom variance in the mixed subject pools studied for language differences.

The role played by the clinician's bias, which emerges from culture-related differences in worldview, sense of self in the world, and so on, also needs to be more clearly understood for its impact on these language and diagnosis studies. The clinician's cultural countertransference (Pérez Foster 1998, Rendon 1996) has been recognized as a formidable influence in the assessment of ethnic groups. Price and Cuellar (1981), in considering the findings of Marcos and colleagues (1973a,b) proposed that because the latter's raters did not possess enough of a bicultural sensibility when assessing their subjects, that the lack accounted for findings that generally differed from other trends in the literature. Gonzales's (1977) work, on the other hand, deliberately investigated the relationship between the cultural background of the rater and the rater's assessment of psychopathology, and found that, regardless of cultural background, raters did not discern any significant differences in the expression of psychopathology in the two language assessments. Clearly, more careful explorations of the interaction between clinician and bilingual patient factors need to be pursued. However, as noted above, these variable diagnostic findings serve to alert the clinician that assessing the bilingual patient is a complex matter. The research predominantly indicates that the language of assessment *does* impact on the manifest expression of psychopathology, although the direction of this effect appears to be variable. I recommend separate assessment in each language for comparison and deliberation.

Second-Language Anxiety and Symptom Variance

Anxiety or pervasive discomfort can accompany the bilingual's clinical presentation in a second language, especially when the bilingual is markedly more proficient in his or her native idioms. The notion of self-expression in a secondarily acquired language as being distant from immediate subjective experience is frequently voiced by patients, and has been entertained from several perspectives by both clinicians and theorists. Distance from experiential truth (Lacan 1977, Rozensky and Gomez 1983), defensive intellectualization of emotion (Buxbaum 1949, Greenson 1950, Marcos 1976, Pérez Foster 1992), and linguistic inaccessibility (Javier 1989, Kolers 1968) have all been cited as explanations for this phenomenon. However, adding to this multilayered veil, as it were, of dulled expression is the further derailing function of the bilingual's anxiety when speaking their nondominant tongue. The notion of appearing passive, inarticulate, simple-minded, or unsophisticated in a second language that one knows is not expressing the full complement of one's thoughts and feelings is anxiety-provoking to many, and depressing to others. Several investigators have noted that, when speaking in their nondominant language, bilinguals perceive themselves as less intelligent and self-confident (Segalowitz 1976). Marcos and Urcuyo (1979) were the first to wisely point out that the monolingual clinician needs to use caution in not misinterpreting the halting quality, sparse words, and emotional preoccupation of the struggling bilingual as psychopathology.

Another related issue to be considered in the English-language assessment of immigrant clients who are from poor and disenfranchised ethnic groups is that the language in which these clients are attempting to express disturbing and charged experiences is in fact the language of the group in power—and thus to some the oppressor. One needs to consider that both the clinician and his or her English symbolize the "other," and that, when viewed in the context of dynamic transferential processes, this type of interaction can evoke sufficient tension to inhibit a host of expressive functions in the patient (Pérez Foster 1998). Viewed from a relational perspective, English, the language of the psychological assessment, may also be the language acquired from this "oppressive other"—the one who begrudgingly tolerates one's stay in their country. Consequently, in relation to this "other," one is cautious, inhibited, unexpressive, passive, and possibly deferential. Learning a second language in repeated relational contexts in which one feels like an inferior self with an intimidating other begins to organize a very particular self configuration that can be subsequently evoked with future English usage.

USING THE MENTAL STATUS EXAMINATION AND PSYCHOSOCIAL HISTORY WITH BILINGUAL CLIENTS

Any individual who presents at a mental health facility in psychological distress is likely to be assessed with procedures that include some form of mental status examination and the recording of a psychosocial history. Considering the potential pitfalls that have just been described in the assessment of bilingual people, I would like to consider these factors as they apply to each one of these assessment formats.

MENTAL STATUS EXAMINATION

Cognitive Sphere

The research that explores the influence of language on the projection of cognitive psychopathology in diagnostic interview has yielded confusing results, to be sure, but stimulates compelling questions regarding the role of language in both the organization and symbolic representation of ideas. All literature cited in this book (except for Gonzales 1977) holds the consensus that, for the bilingual, the language of assessment has some impact on the manifest expression of cognitive pathology. Clinicians should be aware that assessment in the second language can yield confused and regressed cognitive pathology for some bilinguals

(Marcos et al. 1973a,b). However, the majority of clinical and experimental reports denote the exact opposite: that it is in the native language that more regressed psychopathology is manifest (Buxbaum 1949, Del Castillo 1970, Greenson 1950, Javier 1989, Kraph 1955, Laski and Taleporos 1977, Pérez Foster 1992, Price and Cuellar 1981). I recommend separate assessments in each of the patient's languages, with clinicians who are also cognizant of the cultural context of the patient's life and experience. I would encourage the reader to refer to the case of Nina in Chapter 10 of this book as a particular example of second-language use in the service of enhanced cognitive organization. The case also portrays the necessity of bilingual assessment, and the ability of a second language to obfuscate the presence of cognitive pathology that may in fact be quite readily evident in a native language mental status examination.

Affective Sphere

Detached affect, and lack of integration between affect and narrative, are descriptions that have been made of patients who are being assessed in their second language (Bamford 1991). This is noted frequently, but not exclusively, in those who are not proficient second-language speakers. Note should be made to not facilely ascribe these phenomena to the affective blunting that distinguishes more severe pathological states, as intervening linguistic factors may be very much in operation. Marcos and colleagues (1973b) were the first to describe the impact of the "language barrier" in bilinguals on clinical presentation, that is, the level of linguistic deficit involved in processing of information in the nondominant tongue. In comparison with their own native language, nonproficient second language speakers have to exert a more difficult verbalization effort in the nondominant language. Not only do they have less vocabulary at hand and less facility with grammar and word pronunciation, but they are also burdened with the work of constant translation into or from the dominant language (Marcos 1976, Marcos and Alpert 1976,

Marcos and Urcuyo 1979).[3]

In regard to the effects of the language barrier on clinical presentation, authors have reported the bilingual's deflection of both attention and affect onto the more difficult task of encoding in the second language. The result of this deflection has been described as a splitting or lack of integration of experience and emotion. The patient can seem to verbalize upsetting and charged material without the display of appropriate emotion (Balkányi 1964, Marcos 1976). A striking and unfortunate example of this is that bilinguals are frequently misdiagnosed as more depressed when interviewed and assessed in their second language than when assessed in their native tongue (Rendon 1996). Patients speaking in a nondominant language invest extra attention in *how* they say things versus how they *feel* when saying things. They show frequent concern over wording and grammar. It has been noted that for those patients with a ready facility for obsessive mechanisms, the extra cognitive demands of language translation serve to enhance the use of intellectualized defenses, causing even greater emotional distancing from the material (Marcos 1976). In Part III I will be describing the use of these intellectual defenses by the bilingual in various case presentations.

It should also be noted that the emotional coolness and experience-distancing quality of recounting charged or traumatic material in a language other than that of the experience can sometimes serve a facilitating function. Presenting traumatic experience denuded of its full affect in a language unrelated to the experience can at times assist a client in recounting the event

---

3. Linguistic research in the area of second language acquisition notes that various cognitive and linguistic strategies are used by individuals in the process of second language learning, only one of which is literal translation from the dominant language (Grosjean 1982, E. Klein, personal communication 1997). For the purpose of our discussion here, the issue is the subjective and emotional burden of expressing experience in a new and limited language.

without the full potential force of its ego-disruptive charge. I am reminded here of a Middle Eastern woman who upon hospital admission informed me in affective deadpan of the systematic shooting of each of her five family members in front of her when she was age 10. The struggle and effort of translation into English during our interview seemed to contain her, and to consume some of the deep affective edge of her story. However, alone in her room, it was in her native Turkish that she wailed, and attempted to lacerate herself for the crime of surviving. Beginning with the initial diagnostic interview, our sessions in English, because of their affective distance, functioned as a form of titrated entrée into the toxic world of her internal grief. The experience-distant medium of the second language provided for this extremely fragile woman a controlled form of exploring her early trauma—a level of felt experience beyond which she could probably not venture into at the time of her acute hospitalization.

Another example of the occasional facilitating function served by the emotional distance of the second language is provided by a 25-year old Chilean bilingual woman I recently treated who presented with a wide range of inhibitions. The language pattern of her particular treatment followed facile shifting from one language to the other. Just recently sexually active, she began speaking of her first fully aroused sexual experience, with her also Chilean partner, in Spanish. She stopped herself suddenly and said: "I can't handle this; I'm switching to English to tell you this. It sounds much too funky and dirty in Spanish!"

Behavioral Sphere

Functional attributes in the behavioral sphere of bilinguals that may be related to language issues are potential suspiciousness and caution on being in the presence of a stranger. Many clinicians can conjure some personal experience of travel in a country whose language and cultural customs were totally foreign to them. The feeling of vulnerability and the shift toward hyperawareness of external cues are effects we can all relate to to some degree. The trepidation, ambivalence, and conflicted presentation of (especially) those who have poor command of the therapist's language may be due to more than the halting search for words in a foreign language. The fear and frustration of not being understood—especially when such high stakes as psychiatric hospitalization are involved—can be paralyzing for some. For example, a Yugoslavian man was brought into the emergency room of a city hospital to be evaluated psychiatrically after threatening to kill himself. In a difficult interview, he finally said in his halting English, "You don't know me. The only thing you have to tell you whether I am crazy is my words, and I don't speak English that well. So why should I tell you all that I am thinking?" Do we assess this as paranoid suspicion or good reality-testing?

In summary, I would optimally recommend administration of the mental status exam in both the native and second language for the bilingual patient, if staff is available. I would recommend this even for the bilingual who is a proficient English speaker. To avoid bias, these evaluations should be done blindly and then integrated in a team consultation format. These dual-language evaluations would also offer the opportunity to clarify potential discrepancies in interpreting the cultural meaning of certain symptom phenomenology. If dual-language evaluations are not available, and a moderate to poor English speaker is being evaluated, the clinician must remain aware that such characteristics as halting speech, disorganization of ideas, and flattened affect may simply be symptomatic of poor English proficiency, and not necessarily indicators of more serious psychopathology. Also, with regard to diagnostic specificity with the bilingual in general, and given the different clinical picture that might exist in the alternate language system, a conservative posture should probably be maintained until the collection of further data.

THE PSYCHOSOCIAL HISTORY

In the attempt to form a comprehensive developmental context within which to understand a client's presenting psychological distress, clinicians take a psychosocial history, collecting, among other things, information about the client's personal development, the environments in which developmental experiences took place, and the people who played an important part in those environments. We recall that it is specifically on the issue of language and environmental contexts that reconstruction of personal experience may be most affected by language. While the issue of bilingual language organization is complex and still controversial in the field of psycholinguistics, there is a body of research which suggests that separate contexts of language acquisition, that is, cultural settings, can enhance the functional separation of the bilingual's two languages, and, of great interest to the clinician, can render separate streams of associations (Kolers 1968, Lambert et al. 1958, Taylor 1971). These findings stand to have formidable implications for the language in which a bilingual's psychosocial history is taken. The research would suggest the potential for different associations to be aroused by each respective idiom, which has the potential of rendering the reconstruction of respectively different psychosocial products. Typical of this bilingual situation would be the patient whose childhood development spanned a change in environmental locale accompanied by a change in language usage. This situation is optimally represented by the child who spends his or her early years in a native country and language, and who then migrates to a host country and proceeds to adopt both the new culture and new language. Such a situation is presented by the cases of Yulie (Chapter 5), Jan (Chapter 7), and Jean Claude (Chapter 11), all of whom migrated to the United States during their childhood years and adopted new means of both emotional and language functioning in their host environments.

Adding to and confounding the language-related associations produced in a psychosocial history are the basic psychodynamic factors which render a secondarily acquired language an efficient vehicle in the functional repression and emotional isolation of traumatic or conflictual material experienced in the early developmental language. Thus, strong repressive forces which circumscribe the narrative product may also accompany the bilingual's second-language psychosocial history reconstruction.

Given the optimal situation of bilingual language proficiency in mental-health staff, I recommend that the language for psychosocial assessment coincide with the particular segment of developmental history being assessed to ensure that the optimal amount of information is reconstructed as a result of language-specific associational links. When two languages have been an intimate part of early life, both idioms should be used, each language focusing in particular on the segments of development in which that language played a primary functional role. For example, a Chinese male patient who migrated to the United States as a boy of 10 and quickly (as is the case with so many immigrant children) becomes fluent and acculturated in American English–speaking life, will have transacted and symbolically internalized many of his latency experiences, worldly learning, and basic adolescent identifications in English. Many of these experiences would probably be optimally accessed in that language. On the other hand (again, as is the case for so many immigrant children) there is often a "grand divide" in this child's language life: life at home during the latency and adolescent years may have continued to be negotiated, lived, and presumably internalized in Chinese. In a psychosocial narrative, these experiences might very well be best accessed in that language.

It should be noted that, integrated within the developmental data that have been more optimally accessed through use of the phase-specific language, will also be a wealth of information on what I have referred to earlier as "language-bounded self-organizations." These may hold their own particular defensive constellations and operational ego functions, as was graphically portrayed in the case of Yulie. In an assessment, the clinician thus needs to be aware of the contexts of the bilingual's language usage both during development and current functioning. This information can be garnered by integrating the use of the Psycholinguistic History © inquiry (see Chapter 7) within the usual psychosocial history assessment.

In summary, my discussion of language-related factors in psychosocial assessment essentially moves toward the recommendation of dual-language assessments for dual-language lives. While this orientation may already exist as standard fare in many biculturally oriented treatment programs (Guernaccia 1992), the perspective of language-related memory reconstruction and access has not been emphasized. In Chapter 7 I have formulated assessment guidelines that will be of use to the clinician who has no knowledge of the client's developmental language. Not only does the Psycholinguistic History aid in the psychosocial assessment that has just been discussed, tapping information about early and current contextual usage of the respective languages, but it is also able to access the complex psychodynamic functions that dual-language ability serves in the psyche. Exploring the role of bilingualism in self experience, object relationships, and defensive operations, the Psycholinguistic History provides an entrance into the bilingual psyche for both monolingual and bilingual clinicians alike.

7

Taking a
Psycholinguistic History

When the clinician moves beyond the initial level of diagnostic assessment and on to a psychodynamic exploration of presenting problems for the purposes of psychodynamic treatment, there should then follow a serious consideration of the psychodynamic role that language per se plays in the bilingual person's psychic processes. This is to say that integrated within inquiries of both current and psychodevelopmental functioning should be explorations of respective language use in both early and present life. In the academic discipline of psycholinguistics, these inquiries fall within the domains of "language acquisition" and "contexts of utilization" (Grosjean 1982, Hakuta 1986, Vaid 1986). However, in the clinical world, our interests in acquisitional contexts—and early language usage in particular—are in how these factors impact on the internal representation of experience and the dynamics of psychic operations.

In Part I of this book, multiple arguments were developed on both theoretical and clinical grounds, supporting the role of symbolic language in a spectrum of psychodynamic operations. The bilingual's differential use of language was noted to function in the service of psychic defenses, as a mechanism of repression, as a neutralizer of inner desires, and a symbolic signifier of internalized self-representations. Given that early language is learned within important relational contexts, it was argued that words were also the symbolic object-relational capsules of the past. Language is learned within the context of relational matrices. Integrated within the internalized self-object representations of these matrices is the language system through which relationships were lived, experienced, and symbolically internalized. Language can thus signify the self with the other, and all the vicissitudes of life with that other: desires, conflicts, methods of interaction, and defensive inhibitions. And it can signify the spectrum of these psychic dynamics and evoke their developmental origins, as we have seen through transferential enactments in the clinical process. The cases of Anna and Yulie, presented in Chapter 5, were vivid displays of language serving as the dynamic signifier of developmental life. Viewed from a relational perspective, the bilingual speaker possesses not only a dual set of symbols for labeling the external world and internal states, but two separate chains of meaning-producing self-object interactions and developmental contexts.

Whether a second language has been acquired in a different environment or in a different developmental period (in school, upon migration), or whether a second language has simply been taught in early life by another caretaker, each code system will represent a separate composite of unique relational-contextual experiences. At the level of neurocognitive organization, the literature reviewed earlier suggests that many of the cognitive and affective components of these experiences will have been processed and stored in memory along language-specific organizational schema. At the level of psychodynamic organization, these language-specific object experiences may come to be associated with different modes of being, different modes of interacting with another, different modes of discharge, and different modes of experiencing oneself (Pérez Foster 1993a). Clinical reports suggest that the relative isolation or integration of these language-related states is often determined by their conflictual valence. Thus segments of self experience developed through a particular language system, like any other dissociated segment of psychic life, may be dissociated from consciousness in the same way as any other conflictual segment or aspect of the psyche that offers a threat to the general equilibrium

(Bromberg 1996, Harris 1996). However, their concealment from consciousness is maintained through the compounded interaction of two factors: the usual dynamic forces exerted by the defensive mechanisms of repression, isolation, and dissociation; and the "language independence" of the conflictual language-related self-state. Given the literature reviewed in Chapter 3, cognitive access to this language-related state might be limited in a secondarily acquired language unrelated to the original internalized self-experiences, thus compounding the impact of psychic repressive mechanisms. Avoiding the use of a language may thus serve dissociative tendencies in a most efficient way.

ACCESSING THE PSYCHODYNAMICS OF BILINGUALISM

Is there a way for clinicians who have no knowledge of their patients' native languages to assess language-related psychodevelopmental processes? More specifically, is there a way for the clinician to assess whether the bilingual's respective languages serve any psychodynamic function in the patient's current psychic distress? I have organized the Psycholinguistic History (Pérez Foster 1996d; see Table 7–1) as a format of clinical inquiry for this purpose. It explores two spheres of language activity in the bilingual speaker which provide informative approaches to the potential psychodynamic operations of dual-language functioning. The Psycholinguistic History accesses information about:

1. *Psychodevelopmental factors* surrounding each language acquisition. These are the cognitive, affective, behavioral, and object-relational factors associated with the learning of each language. This information can elaborate the role that each language has played in the patient's developing psychic operations, for example, in defensive formations and organization of self experiences.
2. *Current usage factors.* This is information on the current domains of language use, regarding how, when, where,

and with whom the patient's idioms are currently used. This line of inquiry begins to delineate how present language choice is associated with conscious expression of psychic material and manifest personality functioning.

Table 7–1. Psycholinguistic History©

I PSYCHODEVELOPMENTAL FACTORS

1. Age at acquisition of each language.
2. Nature of relationships with people from whom languages were learned.
3. Social/cultural/environmental context of each language acquisition.
4. Psychodevelopmental phase, or special psychodynamic issues surrounding acquisition of each language.
5. Domain or context of each language's early usage.

II CURRENT USAGE FACTORS

1. Current domains or contexts of respective language usage.
2. People to whom languages are spoken.
3. Experience of self when speaking each language.
4. Language of dreams.
5. Language of fantasies and internal self-talk.

Copyright © R. Pérez Foster 1996. Adopted from Pérez Foster 1996d by permission of the author and Jason Aronson Inc.

I would like to illustrate use of this inquiry format with a case example that accompanied original description of the Psycholinguistic History in 1996.

The Case of Jan

Jan is a 37-year-old Scandinavian man who came to the United States on a graduate fellowship at age 25 and never returned home. He eventually acquired a Ph.D. in epidemiology and married an American woman. His English is perfect. He is a respected researcher in his particular area, but is also involved in commercial real estate investments from which he makes a substantial income. He is part of a business consortium with fellow countrymen. Jan presented with intense hypochondriasis, fear of death, and the compulsion to check his heartbeat. He also complained of explosive rages toward his business partners. In time, he described his "other compulsion": frequenting prostitutes who are "putty in my hands; they are willing to silently obey all of my sexual demands." Jan began this activity shortly after divorcing his first wife.

The patient is the second oldest of five children. He has an older brother and three significantly younger sisters. He remembers his father as emotionally removed and unapproachable. His mother was his everything. "She was my world—I could not live or breathe without her." From ages 4–7, his mother would take Jan in to bathe with her. "I was imprisoned by her touches, her smells, and an excitement that I did not know what to do with. Then when I am 7, the first of three baby girls is born, and she drops me like I am a nothing. I didn't know whether to feel relief or like murdering her."

Early latency years are difficult for Jan. He is shy and has trouble separating from mother and home. He idolizes his older brother and male cousins; however, they call him sissy and do not include him in their games. Around age 10 Jan begins to come into his own, excelling at school and making some friends. Adolescence proves difficult, however, as his mother is intrusive and demanding. "She chases away my girl friends." At university, Jan again excels in the academic sphere, but is inhibited in his social relationships. He blames this on the fact that he still lives at home with his family. Upon graduation, he is offered a fellowship by an international health organization to pursue research in the United States. "I have my chance to finally get away from my mother. I come to America and never go back."

Jan's Psycholinguistic History

I. Psychodevelopmental Factors

The first four items of this section of the history can be explored jointly:

1. *The ages of language acquisition.*
2. *The relationships to the people who taught each language.*
3. *The social/cultural/environmental context of each language acquisition.*
4. *Any remarkable psychodevelopmental issues surrounding the language acquisition periods.*

Jan learns his first language from his mother. It was the language of his early infantile developmental life, his intimate relationship with his mother, and the protracted period of overstimulation with her. An important fact is that English is spoken by the father and older brother, but mainly reserved for use outside the home in business and academic domains.

At age 10 Jan also acquires English. He is fluent in only eight months' time. The circumstances surrounding his English acquisition are quite notable. Jan develops a warm paternal relationship with his English instructor, who tells him that he will excel in the new language and possibly become more fluent than his brother. From this moment on, Jan vows to speak only English, to think in English, and to count in English. Indeed he does this. The patient claims that this single statement from his instructor was the turning point of his life.

5. The domain of early language usage.

Jan reserved his new English for use at school and in newfound interchange with his brother and father. "Through English I finally excelled, felt like a man, and became like my brother. It was the one way in which I could compete." As Jan worked with these issues in treatment, he came to realize that English was a vehicle he used to identify with the men in his life. But at an even deeper level, thinking in a newfound English speaking world—a world uncontaminated by his mother's tongue—seems to have also offered Jan a fairly comprehensive defensive framework through which he could isolate and split off his early trauma with her. Thinking in a new symbolic system was not unlike a dissociative mechanism. Thus maintaining the psychic disruption of his early years at bay, he managed to use his latency years in the service of developing functions and skills that would serve him in later life. We note here the powerful role that language plays for this patient in the development of defensive structures and the organization of his self-experience.

II. Current Language Usage

The reader is reminded that this patient eventually left his motherland, trained as an academic researcher in the United States, and came to live an Americanized lifestyle. What is the fate of the patient's language usage within his current adult adjustment, and what part, if any, does it play in how he organizes the expression of his psychic distress? This section of the Psycholinguistic History will assess the patient's current language choice and contextual usage.

1. *In what domains are Jan's languages currently used?*
2. *To whom are the languages spoken?*
3. *What is Jan's experience of self speaking and negotiating life in each language?*
4. *In what language does he dream?*
5. *In what language does he fantasize and self-talk?*

1 and 2: languages currently used and to whom they are spoken.

Jan lives a tightly constructed English-speaking life with his current second wife and American friends. He writes for English language scientific journals. His spoken English is precise and accompanied by polished manners and emotional restraint. He uses his native language *only* when conducting business with his investment partners. Here his interactions are marked with more spontaneity, lack of verbal caution, and above all verbal rages when he does not get his way. In fact this has become a problem; aggressive negotiating has turned into bullying and near physical fighting. "I will let no one take me for a sucker," he says.

3: language-related experience of self.

In his English-speaking world, Jan consciously feels quite a success, proud of his American life, social status, and the elitism of his academic circle. However, it is in his native language that the deep emotional doubts about his worth and manliness are keenly experienced and acted upon. The patient and I have come to understand the fighting in the workplace as the transference of the aggressive struggle with his brother and father. It is his rage at their shunning him and leaving him to be sissified and exploited by his mother. He wants to kill them for this, still. Speaking in the native tongue with his countrymen consistently evokes this transference. The music, mood, and meaning of the first language pulls Jan closest to the lived experience of feeling like an unmanly boy-child. In the second language he is able to defensively avoid these painful aspects of his self experience, both by the real competitive success that his English-speaking life affords, and by the second language's powerful defensive ability to affectively neutralize, intellectualize, and/or isolate the early conflictual experiences he "lived" in the mother tongue.

4 and 5: language of dreams, fantasies, and internal self-talk.

Turning to Jan's internal life, simple inquiry into the language of his sexual fantasies reveals that they are always in his native idiom. Most of his fantasies are organized around the sexual trauma with his mother. On the English-speaking surface his interpersonal and sexual approach to his wife is tentative. However, internally it is only the voices of his early life that fully arouse him as they depict some configuration of a physical sadomasochistic fantasy. Indeed, his activities with prostitutes who are "putty in my hands," are a repetitive enactment of his mother holding him captive in the bath—this time with Jan as the captor.

In summary, Jan is a complicated man whose early developmental trauma has deeply affected his object relations, impulse control, and organization of self. Indeed, his presentation of sexual and physical enactments (hypochondriasis, rages, sadomasochistic enactments) embodied repetitive and desperate efforts at self-restoration (Stolorow and Atwood 1991). His analysis will have to proceed like any other: with an ultimate understanding of his deep desires, a working through of his traumas and their impact on his self and relational worlds, and the ultimate elaboration of new psychic mechanisms. However, from his psycholinguistic history we learn that his most conflictual desires and traumata are deeply associated with his infantile language. They are still embedded in his native language when he rails at his colleagues, or fantasizes and acts out a sadomasochistic encounter.

Interpreting to Jan that he uses his English to guard against the emergence of these deep and dangerous feelings is useful and effective as a clarifying intervention. But the real question in this treatment, and the treatment of any other bilingual patient, is to what depth Jan can work through this early material in English, the language of his resistance. In effect, his mother language is a condensed capsule of the most affectively laden and cognitively detailed desires, fears, and rages of his early life. Jan agrees to as he says "go into my language." But how do we in the context of the therapeutic dyad enter this language system, given the fact that I do not speak Swedish (a factor which most decidedly sides with the patient's resistance), and that accessibility to Jan's early language-specific experiences is also clearly impacted by repressive mechanisms? In Chapter 8 I will be describing various methods of entering the client's language world, however at this point I would like to offer the interesting course taken by Jan's treatment.

Jan has begun to tell his dreams and to recount his rages in his native language (which he later translates). The level of clear emotion that this evoked was fruitful for the work. The patient also used another unique vehicle. Initially unaware of the determinism behind his actions, Jan began a research project that involved a population from his own country: the study of sexually transmitted diseases in young children. This work basically involved reading journal reports of children who had been sexually abused. It was through this unique project that Jan was finally able to enter his mother's language, as well as her bath, ultimately reconstructing the repressed memories of his sexualized experiences with her.

Jan has become increasingly aware of the duality that exists in his psychological life. The therapeutic work thus far has made him quite conscious of the role that his English life plays in binding his anxiety and diffusing his impulses. It has taken years for him to utter the words of his first language in session: "It's too much like this—too powerful." He then goes back to English. I believe that the "power" he speaks of is not only the affective accuracy and intensity of the mother language, but the potential strength of the transference enactments that might also be evoked when he enters the primal sensorial space of his mother's speech. Thus far the patient and I have been coasting productively on the positive wave of being two brothers, analyzing and telling stories in English—Jan's language of being adult, equal, and strong. But there are other unspoken dimensions of coexperience brewing between us. I can feel

Jan bristle when I remind him about a late payment. Also, I experience my own countertransference as I resist his petulant demands for time changes and make-up sessions. I know that I am fighting against becoming "putty in [his] hands." [Pérez Foster 1996d, pp. 256–260]

I would like to conclude by making several points. Language is a powerful organizer of experience. It becomes intimately yoked to the objects associated with the language learning, to the environmental ambience in which the language learning took place, and to the internal psychodevelopmental state of the child at the time of acquisition. When several languages are acquired, and especially when they are learned within different relationships and different developmental contexts, *each language code becomes a kind of signifier* for that set of lived experiences. As we saw with Jan, who acquired his second language under very special developmental circumstances, English became a powerful signifier of new identifications, ego ideals, defensive structures, and autonomous ego functions. Thus, one might say that in the multilingual individual, language can serve as a characterological organizer. In the face of early trauma or unresolved early conflict, the clinician must also be aware that bilingualism can serve a highly dynamic and defensive function, for a second language system is a formidable binder of anxiety that can effectively isolate and dissociate affect initially experienced in another language system.

Foreign-born patients who enter our consulting rooms citing the often-heard immigrant's adage; "starting a new life in a new country," are wiser and more complex than we give them credit for. However, monolingual clinicians can now begin to access their patients' language-related identifications, defensive functions, relational experiences, and modes of organizing psychic distress through inquiry into their psycholinguistic histories. [Pérez Foster 1996d, pp. 260–261]*

---

*Copyright © 1996 by Jason Aronson Inc., and reprinted by permission.

The Case of Marika

Marika is a 59-year-old woman who entered treatment upon her engagement to a fellow countryman from Eastern Europe who, like her, had been a survivor of the Holocaust. Marika met Simon, her fiancé, in a group for hidden children of the Holocaust that she has attended for two years. "After so many years of living inside of a deep cave, I have come out again. This man undoes me. I don't know what to do with myself. Should I follow how I feel with him?"

Marika recounts that just prior to meeting her fiancé she had been extremely depressed following the death of her husband and the move of her daughter to another city. She had been treated with antidepressants and encouraged at that time to join the survivor's group. Marika stated that her current losses seemed "to have done me in after a long life where I have managed to survive losing so much." Marika was referring to the loss of her father and grandparents in the Holocaust. Marika, her mother, and two sisters had managed to survive by being hidden in safehouses until their complexly orchestrated passage to Paraguay when she was age 12. Marika did not clearly know that her father and grandparents had been exterminated in a concentration camp until she was a young adult. Her mother, for complex reasons which included sparing her children the horrors of their history, never told them of the father's capture and death, preferring to maintain the story that the father had run off with his mistress.

A strange mixture of denial and confabulation pervaded Marika's household and her adolescent years in Paraguay. Included in the adjustment to this new life was the pressure to learn Spanish and not use the native language. The mother insisted that the small family of women start fresh and never speak of the painful past; Marika was never offered the opportunity to understand what had happened to them. She says that there was a period of time when she did not speak at all. "Eventually I made some kind of a life, followed what people told me to do, and spoke Spanish. Because I did well at school and people seemed to like me, my mother thought that this meant I was happy. Boys seemed to like me; this impressed my mother even more."

In her later teens, Marika began to fantasize about living in the United States. She applied to and was accepted at an American college. She states that her years as a college student in the United States began to open new hopes for her. She had already known some English, quickly became proficient, and began to feel that maybe she would really begin to make some choices in her life. She excelled in her chosen area, chemistry; entered pharmacy school, and met her first husband there, an indigenous Latin American. In terms of her social and ethnic affiliation, Marika identified as a bilingual Latin American who, especially in her early years in the United States, tried as much as possible to eschew the small group of Paraguayan Jews who, like herself, had emigrated to the United States. "In my soul, though, I didn't know where the hell I belonged."

Marika's marriage soon ended in divorce, however, after her first clinical depression. About her husband, Marika states: "We drifted apart; I frankly don't even know what drew us together." She describes her depression as having been precipitated by the birth of her child, and a violent confrontation with her mother in which Marika forced her to tell the truth about her father's disappearance.

Marika focused on raising her child, and advancing in her career. She describes a mild but chronic dysphoria throughout her middle years, punctuated by bouts of more acute symptoms for which she is treated with medication. Marika married again "for companionship, not for love. I don't think I know what that is." This time she married a Latin American man who is also Jewish. The marriage is short-lived, however, as her husband dies of a heart attack just after their third anniversary. Her ensuing depressive re-

action leads her to seek pharmacologic treatment again, find
the Holocaust survivors group, and eventually seek an analytic treatment with me. At this time she has just become
engaged to her fiancé.

Marika enters her individual treatment with the stated
wish of "discussing my love problems with a woman, and fig-
uring them out once and for all." She shifts her narrative
easily between English and Spanish. Fresh from explorations
in her survivors group, she shares her rage toward her
mother who so distorted the events of her father's death.
She had loved her father deeply, and mourned his loss
quietly, not daring to show her feelings to a mother whose
own reactions she could not understand. Marika also has
periods of recouping from her anguish by soberly surmis-
ing that her mother's only way of coping with the insanity
of the Holocaust was to construct a story that had some
semblance of familiarity to it. "After all, my mother always
suspected my father's affair. I think she spoiled me for men,
though. I don't know how to love them."

At this point in the treatment, Marika begins to explore
her tremendous attraction to Simon, his loving nature, and
most importantly the comfort that he affords when speaking his heavily accented English, which is always accentuated
with words from their country. Marika says that she has not
spoken her native language since going to Paraguay. It is
apparent that, throughout her middle years, Marika has
slowly moved toward her identification with her Jewish past,
the reconstruction of her early life, and the tragic loss of
her father. The transference to Simon and to her group will
be important elements to work through in the treatment.

Marika's Psycholinguistic History

I. Psychodevelopmental Factors

The first four items of this section of the history can be explored
jointly:

1. *The ages of language acquisition.*
2. *Nature of relationships to the people from whom languages were learned.*
3. *Social/cultural/environmental context of each language acquisition.*
4. *Psychodevelopmental phase, or special psychodynamic issues surrounding acquisition of each language.*

Marika learns her first language from her parents and extended family at a time in the family's history when it is nurturing and intact. Her European language is the symbolic idiom of her early infantile life and the deep internalizations of her primary objects. It is also the language through which so much of her loss of father, extended family, and countryland was symbolized. It is the language of her Holocaust, and the terrors of hiding and escape. Spanish, on the other hand, learned at age 12 in South America, was the language of denial of her historical past up to that time. Force-fed to her by the pressures of a new school context and a mother who was immersed in the aggressive suppression of her own losses, Spanish became the medium through which Marika "walked through [her] life in silence." Spanish was also the language of her experimental adolescence, an idiom of discovery for her talents in the natural sciences, her social poise in peer situations, and her flirtatious ease with boys.

Marika begins to teach herself English on her own around age 16 with the fantasy that she will live in the United States someday, a place that is a new start. She totally immerses herself in English language life upon her beginning college in the United States. Marika feels that this language begins to express a new self who is in control of her life for the first time. She negotiates a physical separation from her mother and functions autonomously during her college years and at the beginning of her life as an adult woman.

5. Domains or context of each language's early usage.

Monolingual in her European native language until the age of 12, Marika essentially stops speaking upon her arrival to South America. There is thus no open discourse, verbal mourning, or reconstruction of her traumatic events with a mother who discourages these actions and insists on conversation in the new Spanish language. Marika is left with silent talk within herself, which she says slowly deteriorates to no language at all. She is in fact silent for a time[4] until she learns conversational Spanish. Spanish usage during the years in Paraguay pervades all social life and academic learning. Marika states that it is a language which she has never really used to divulge her feelings or anything significant about the facts and details of her life. English, however, voluntarily chosen and freshly learned at the brink of her adulthood, creates a new medium for her, devoid of both the trauma that resonates in her European tongue, and the aggressive denial that pervades her secondly acquired Spanish. "I can finally practice saying what I want in English."

II. Current Usage Factors

We recall that Marika settles in the United States and identifies socially as a Spanish- and English-speaking Latin American woman. Her social network includes Americans and Latin Americans of both indigenous and Jewish European origin. Her two marriages have been to bilingual Latin American men. She works as a pharmacist in New York City.

This section of the Psycholinguistic History will assess the patient's current language choices and contextual usage:

1. Current domains or contexts of respective language usage.

---

4. Eva Hoffman, in her autobiographical account of her migration from Poland to Canada as a child, *Lost in Translation* (1989), likewise describes her empty period without words.

2. *People to whom languages are spoken.*
3. *Experience of self when speaking each language.*
4. *Language of dreams.*
5. *Language of fantasies and internal self-talk.*

1, 2, and 3: languages currently used, who they are spoken to, and the language-related experience of self, can be considered jointly.

> Marika uses English and Spanish interchangeably in her social and work life. She reports being more full-ranged in her affective expression in English and more formal in Spanish. Life with her two Latin American husbands was negotiated bilingually but pervaded by a formality and distance beyond which she says "we did not go." Marika associates her experience of self, while interchanging in Spanish, with the years of her South American life in which only the "surface" was important. "I know how to behave and what is expected of me when I am in my Spanish, but I think that I am also cold. In English I never know exactly what is going to happen, or come out of me; I'm easier." Recently Marika has begun to use some phrases of her old European language with Simon. She speaks of being unsure about both her pronunciation and herself while speaking, but it has provided an extremely enjoyable aspect to their relationship, and she thinks it may even provide a large source of her attraction to her fiancé.

4 and 5: language of dreams, self-talk, and fantasy.

> Marika's dream life has always been a spectrum of three-language experience. Her dreams, she says, were the only clue that her native language had not totally disappeared. Typically she could never remember her dreams, but she would know when she had dreamed in her native language because the "sound" of it would stay with her "like when people are talking in another room and you can't understand the words but can hear the sounds of it." Since joining the survivors

group, Marika has realized that many group members dreamed about the Holocaust years; she was not sure whether she did or not. About her internal life, Marika states that she "trained" herself in English self-talk. Once she came to the United States she wanted to wipe away her "Spanish falseness" (the way she had tried to wipe away her trauma). Interestingly, Marika's sexual fantasies were of being seduced by a Spanish-speaking man, with whom she flirted like an innocent girl, almost but never quite reaching the point of consummation. These fantasies have stopped since being engaged to Simon.

Marika's use of three languages in her psychic life presented quite a challenge for me as I was only conversant in two of them. From her Psycholinguistic History, I had surmised that the Spanish language (and culture) had provided quite a formidable defensive matrix for her. It furnished a new symbolic meaning system that was devoid of deep connection to her trauma, as well as a formal set of female-gendered behaviors whose coquettishness belied the pain of a girl who had lost her early life. Indeed, these dynamics were clearly reflected in Marika's language-related transference projections as she avoided encroaching attachment to me. During our fairly open English interchanges, she would deftly switch to Spanish and literally freeze me out through formal conversational tones, narrowed facial expression, and the infusion of a strong countertransferential injunction to not move any closer to her. Upon much later analysis of this transference defense, Marika understood that this had been the basic posture that she had maintained with her Latin husbands, which ended, she felt, in their ultimately leaving her: "sealing myself like a tomb. Becoming *una muñeca* (a doll) was the only way that I could live after losing my father and grandparents." Difficult and moving junctures in the treatment are moments when Marika is at a true loss for words. Losing her Spanish and English, she simply bears her anguish, finding no words as of yet in her native language to verbalize what she feels. The relationship with

Simon is moving her closer to her early language, as her transference to him very much evokes elements of her early life, her father's love, and the trauma of all her losses. Given my lack of ability to speak Marika's European language, I don't know how far I will be able to move with her into the deeper areas of her interior and her terrifying experiences in the Holocaust. We will see. However, her treatment thus far is serving to analyze and work through the use of her complex language system in binding the disintegrating impact of her trauma. This was a language-related psychodynamic system which impressively pervaded multiple facets of Marika's external character and deeper elements of her defensive psychic structure. Marika's work with the survivors group is a tremendous step toward reconnecting with her losses and finally discoursing with others about what has happened to all of them. This was precisely what her mother never allowed, and which the Spanish life further buried. Marika has now stopped using Spanish with me in session.

8

Using Bilingual Translators

In agency and institutional settings in particular, the situation often arises where a client who speaks little or no English presents in need of assessment. Mental health practice in large metropolitan areas is at times able to appropriately rise to this need, possessing within its systems facilities that offer integrated bilingual and bicultural services, or clinics that are focused and funded for the express purpose of servicing a particular ethnic group (Guernaccia 1992). In the New York metropolitan area, this latter category is represented for example by the Bilingual Treatment Program for Hispanic patients at the Bellevue Hospital Center, the Russian Psychological and Socialization Program of the New Hope Guild, and the Chinese Manpower Agency. These programs represent the best of mental health services delivery, where professional staff is clinically, culturally, and linguistically prepared to assess and treat an ethnic client on a footing as competent as any other clinical facility.

However, in many cases a facility is not prepared with the clinical staff needed to service the large members of multiethnic clients who seek services, and what ensues is an awkward set of activities. Bluntly put, clinicians literally "scramble" in these cases, scouring the facility for translators of whatever language is needed at the moment. Clinicians make use of other health-care workers, support staff, maintenance crew, strangers in the waiting room, or relatives that the client may have brought in tow. Needless to say, using such translators produces extremely compromised clinical and ethical situations where the potential for inaccuracy and distortion is great, and the danger of breaching confidentiality is poorly controlled.

At this time there seem to exist no formal set of clinical standards for the use of translators in mental health situations that are grounded in parameters from the academic literature, or methodological approaches that have been developed and used by other related disciplines. The current state of the mental health literature specific to the use of translators is small[5] and presents sometimes conflicting suggestions. Furthermore, there are yet no formal standards for the training of bilingual translators in mental health settings. This is of particular concern because there are reports of alarming consequences that have emerged from translated psychiatric assessments in which patient safety and care have been compromised (Price 1975, Sabin 1975, Vazquez and Javier 1991). In his study of the use of translators at Bellevue and Gouverneur hospitals in New York City, Marcos (1979) found that "clinicians evaluating non-English-speaking patients through an interpreter are confronted with consistent, clinically relevant, interpreter-related distortions which may give rise to important misconceptions about the patient's mental status" (p. 173). Berkanovic (1980) and Holden and Serrano (1989) highlight similar issues in the public health and medical arenas. In this chapter I would like to accomplish a threefold task: review the reported problems on the use of clinical translators so that clinicians are clearly aware of the relevant factors involved, propose a comprehensive set of guidelines for how the clinician should use a translator in the clinical situation, and propose an operational guide for the formal training of translators in the mental health setting.

---

5. Baker 1981, Baxter and Cheng 1996, Bradford and Muñoz 1993, Cannon 1983, Freed 1988, Glasser 1983, Ishisaki et al. 1985, Kline et al. 1980, MacKinnon and Michels 1971, Marcos 1979, Price 1975, Richie 1964, Sabin 1975, Vazquez and Javier 1991, Westermeyer 1987, 1990.

USING A BILINGUAL TRANSLATOR—
PROBLEMATIC ISSUES

Who is a bilingual translator in the mental health setting? Unfortunately, the answer to this is "anyone." My own exposure to a variety of clinical settings, and information garnered from the literature, both indicate that bilingual translators span a wide range of competence and appropriateness for the job. They generally fall into two categories:

1. *Trained bilingual mental-health workers.* These are clinical or paraprofessional mental health staff who are balanced bilinguals in English and another language, and who have been offered some instruction on the translation process and its role in the clinical situation. There are no official standards for translators in the clinical field; thus, the level of sophistication in translation ability is left to the discretion of the individual agency. I have personally trained bilingual mental-health translators who include high school-educated community workers, agency support staff, college students, professional translators, and an array of multidisciplinary clinicians. Basic elements in their instruction include directives on strict maintenance of confidentiality on material divulged in session; some education on general psychic functioning and the cognitive anomalies that are common to patients in emotional distress; and, in the model that I favor, instruction in their role as language translators versus interpreters of the patient's meanings. (I will expand on this below.)

2. *Untrained bilinguals enlisted from the immediate setting.* These are untrained and unknown bilingual translators quickly enlisted to service by pressured clinicians, who pose a threat to both the patient and the basic integrity of the clinical situation. Untrained translators are often confused about their role, tend to minimize psychopathology, and tend to personally interpret the narratives of the

client (Marcos 1979, Vazquez and Javier 1991, Westermeyer 1990). The discourse of a patient who is affectively
labile, confused, disorganized, or tangential in his or her
thinking is admittedly difficult to translate. Untrained
translators will tend to want to "clean up" and "make
sense" of the cognitive distortions, thus adding their own
interpretations to the patient's verbalizations. This makes
it extremely difficult for the clinician to make an accurate assessment of cognitive processes in a mental status
exam.

In addition, translators who are unknown to the clinician,
and untrained in the parameters of their role, can carry their
own personal agendas into the translation situation. The following example demonstrates this issue. A bilingual Dominican man
who worked as an agency's doorman was enlisted several times
by clinicians as a Spanish-English translator. He had been a resi-
dent of the United States for ten years. Clinicians began to notice, however, a tendency on his part to exaggerate the antiso-
cial behavior (e.g., drug use, promiscuity) in several Dominican
patients for whom he had served as translator. When questioned
about his views, he openly expressed his prejudice against recently arrived immigrants from his own country, whom he saw
as lower class and inferior to himself. His own possible struggle
with an identification that he wanted to deny emerged in the
form of hostile judgments and distortions of clients' disclosures
during translation.

The problem of an untrained translator's subjective interference is even further exaggerated by the common use of family members as translators in institutional settings. Their own
subjective biases, identification with the patient, and integral role
in the patient's family system often serve not only to potentially
distort translated narrative, but also inhibit the patient in fuller
expression. Needless to say, the use of a patient's child for translation—which happens more often than we would like to think—
is probably one of the worst examples of a translation dyad, given

the child's extreme vulnerability at witnessing the parent in distress, and the parent's probable conflict in exposing their distress during the interview. The use of relatives as translators, in my view, should be avoided (Freed 1988, MacKinnon and Michels 1971).

Among clinicians who assess nonproficient English speakers, or who do so with the aid of unreliable translators, anecdotally voiced concerns over misdiagnosis and the fear of misassessing risk situations are common. I strongly encourage clinicians to publish these precarious clinical situations as a call for clinical standards in the preparation of translators for mental-health settings. Vazquez and Javier (1991) recently published several such vignettes, one of which included translated misassessment of suicidality in a female patient. A stunning report made by Sabin in 1975 described the suicide of two Spanish-speaking patients evaluated by English-speaking psychiatrists with the aid of a translator. Sabin delineated his view that "the patient's emotional suffering may be selectively underestimated when the clinician works by means of translation" (p. 197). He added the warning that translated evaluation of a patient may give undue prominence to cognitive processes "at the expense of full recognition of the patient's affective despair" (p. 198).

Writers have noted some clinicians' general subjective discomfort and probable anxiety upon the use of a translator in the clinical interview. The clinician can feel vulnerable, potentially threatened by the translator, and generally concerned that he or she will not be able to "get to the patient" (MacKinnon and Michels 1971, p. 453). In an interesting assessment and comparison of both the patient's and clinician's respective reactions to the use of a translator in an initial interview, Kline et al. (1980) found that patients interviewed with translators felt understood, helped, and wanted to return. The clinicians, on the other hand, felt that the same patients who had been interviewed with translators had *not* felt understood, and probably did not want to return for further evaluation. The authors viewed these findings as a powerful example of clinicians' projection of their own discomfort at not being effective in reaching their patients in the presence of a translator. Kline and colleagues (1980) make yet another call for the mental health field to formally integrate into clinical training factors that relate to the clinician's reactions to cross-cultural situations.

DEFINING THE ROLE OF A BILINGUAL TRANSLATOR

Close reading of the literature on the translator in the mental-health setting shows the translator in a variety of functions which merit some distinction. Writers such as Baker (1981), Cannon (1983), Freed (1988), Kinzie (1985), and others view the translator as not simply a literal interpreter of language, but rather as a cultural representative who can interpret culture-specific meanings and nuances to the therapist. Using known translators who are usually members of the same ethnic group as the client being evaluated, these clinicians place the translator in a position that exerts substantive influence on the clinical situation. Other writers such as de Zulueta (1990) and Ishisaki et al. (1985) essentially ascribe a co-therapist function to the translator. Cannon (1983) in addition views the translator as a bridge between therapist and client, someone who can ease the ethnic client's discomfort at being in the presence of an ethnic stranger. She in fact conceived of the translator as an "authority" for the client who can help them understand, be understood, and behave in a socially acceptable manner during session (p. 13).

I in fact do not favor this latter perspective and find it somewhat demeaning of the client. Also, the onus of "adjusting" to the cross-cultural strangeness of the clinical situation is potentially placed on the client, who is already under pressure and distress. There seems to be no responsibility given to the clinician here to struggle with the process of understanding his or her client, and behaving in a way that is comfortable and syntonic to that client. Contemporary clinical literature on the dynamics of cross-cultural dyads, such as the work of Ibrahim, (1985) and

Tyler et al. (1985) in fact encourage both clinician and client to struggle through queries about each other's cultural differences, and in the process of this interchange create connection and dynamic interaction between each other.

The use of translators as both linguistic and cultural "interpreters" in fact presents many potential pitfalls. A pervasive one is the translator's tendency to impose subjective opinions and assessments of the client's discourse. Vazquez and Javier (1991) point out that instead of functioning as channels for the client's narrative to the therapist, mental-health translators at times lose their perspective and behave as interviewers. The translated material offered to the clinician thus emerges as the distilled yield of the translator's interpretation (albeit a culturally sensitive one!). For these reasons, in the mental-health context, I prefer the term *translator* to *interpreter*. Interpreter is a rather loaded word in the clinical world, for it implies more than a translator of language symbols; it suggests an interpreter of meaning, which I view as the unique purview of the clinician-client dyad.

I would like at this point to describe my own position on the use of translators. In my work and in the training of others, I emphasize the absolute primacy of the patient–therapist dyad, and use the translator as a fairly technical vehicle or adjunct to the clinical situation. I de-emphasize the use of the translator as a personal presence, preferring to struggle with the client myself in the intersubjective space of nonverbal communication and at-present experience with them. If I need a "cultural" explanation of something, I simply ask the client for it. I direct the translator to maintain the designation of the patient's voice at all times ("direct translation"), and reject any reversals (Bradford and Muñoz 1993). For example, for a translator to say: "She says '*she*' has trouble sleeping" is not acceptable. In the voice of the patient, the translation should be "*I* have trouble sleeping." Following an approach similar to the one used by Bradford and Muñoz (1993) in the treatment situation (which will be discussed later in the chapter), I use the style of *concurrent* versus *sequen-*

tial translation to minimize the translator's own imposition of phrasal emphasis or thematic pauses. This, in addition to *direct translation* (i.e., the literal word-to-word rendering of the patient's discourse), gives me a better sense of the patient's own thought processes. If I need idiomatic interpretation of a turn of words that is unfamiliar to me, I ask the patient what the words mean. I find that the translator's tendency to condense or summarize the patient's sequential phrases, and/or add their own meanings (Bradford and Muñoz 1993, Vazquez and Javier 1991) is much decreased with these general directives. In addition, the common tendency to leave out translated elements of a narrative because of the recency effect[6] caused by sequential phrase translation (Bradford and Muñoz 1993) or the translator's own personal choice of material is lessened as well.

Notwithstanding the structural directives that can be imposed on a translated clinical interview to "optimize" the subjective voice of the non-English-speaking patient, and "minimize" the subjective voice of the translator, one cannot blind oneself to the power and influence of the bilingual "language-keeper" in the room. Roy (1992), in her sociolinguistic analysis of the parameters of interpreted dialogue, clearly demystifies the notion of interpreter as a mere "robotic conduit of information" (p. 21). Instead, she graphically demonstrates the subtle power of the interpreter in the three-way interaction, as he or she interprets others' intentions, creates ground rules for turn-taking, and projects their own perceptions of the social situation in the room.[7] We psychodynamic clinicians would view these conversational behaviors as the projection of inner psychic determinants,

---

6. The *recency effect is* part of the spectrum of serial position phenomena observed in the memory recall of items in a narrative. The location of data within the narrative seems to be an important variable, such that items at the end are recalled with greater frequency than items in the middle (Glanzer and Cunitz 1966).

7. See also Tannen (1984, 1989) for sociolinguistic perspectives on conversational interactions.

or the expressions of intersubjective communication. However, the point here is that students of dialogic processes from various domains all acknowledge the formidable influence of the translator—a factor that clinicians need to consider and integrate even though they may have imposed structural parameters on the translator's functions.

USE OF TRANSLATORS IN THE PSYCHOTHERAPY SITUATION

I support the use of translators for assessment, diagnostic, and evaluative purposes. However, I do not favor the use of translators for most psychotherapy situations, especially those of a psychodynamic nature. My perspective is admittedly a subjective one based on my experience, in clinical practice and supervision, that the procedure is not particularly effective. I would venture to say that the use of a translator in a psychodynamic or psychoanalytically oriented treatment approach would almost be untenable considering the myriad intersubjective facets of communication, multiple dual transference projections, and the complex linguistic parameters of psychic organization that would all have to be analyzed for the reconstructive work of the analytic treatment to proceed.

Bradford and Muñoz (1993) have published an impressive seminal report on a psychotherapy with a Spanish-speaking woman. Their report also includes valuable descriptions on the use of translators in general clinical situations that have been influential in my own work and amply cited in this chapter. However, I must unfortunately part ways with these authors on their view of their translator-assisted psychotherapy work as really "psychodynamic." Close inspection of their cited goals for the treatment include catharsis, cognitive reframing, medical education, and strengthening of already existing adaptive defenses and coping skills. These are hallmark goals for a basic supportive psychotherapy, which by definition must function within the framework of an extremely positive transference. This transference

remains rather fixed throughout the treatment on the projected image of the therapist as an approving and validating figure.
The therapeutic efficacy and clinical appropriateness of this treatment is clear from the report, notwithstanding the caveats cited
by the authors on not comparing translated psychotherapy to
traditional psychotherapy where the dyad speaks the same language. However, I would be cautious about describing their translated psychotherapy as really "psychodynamic" as it does not at
all involve the development, enactment, and subsequent analysis of the conflicting and complex transference formations that
are inherent to the psychodynamic therapeutic process. In addition, there is no recognition of potential transference projections
toward the translator, who can be as much an object of the
patient's fantasies as the therapist. This creates a transference–
countertransference triad, as it were, producing many points of
intersubjective connection at both conscious and unconscious
levels of experience. In a true psychodynamic treatment, these
dynamics would all have to be worked through—a formidable
job considering its complexity and the cumbersomeness of the
translation situation. Baxter and Cheng (1996) recently reporting on a psychodynamic therapy of a Chinese patient with a
translator, note the significant difficulties inherent in such a
process, and the compromised treatment goals that ensued in
their own clinical work.

I side with both Bradford and Muñoz (1993) and Baxter and
Cheng (1996) in the need to explore the parameters of the translated therapeutic situation; however my own view is that translators are more applicable to the evaluative and assessment end
of the clinical spectrum, except for possible application with
treatment interventions that are much more cognitive, behavioral, or instructional in nature, and that operate at conscious
levels of experience. Such interventions have already been described by counselors of the deaf, vocational rehabilitation counselors, and independent-living skills trainers (Harvey 1982, 1989,
Hittner and Bornstein 1990, Shapiro and Harris 1976).

GUIDELINES FOR USE OF TRANSLATORS
IN CLINICAL INTERVIEWS

I would like to offer the following guidelines to the monolingual clinician who may use a bilingual translator in the process of a clinical assessment interview. We understand that the level of translator competence and clinical awareness will be extremely variable, and that many translators will have received no preparation or training at all. I want to make clear my position of viewing the translator as neither an interpreter of the patient's meanings, nor a co-interviewer with me. Rather, I view the translator as a channel through which the patient and I can conduct our discourse. I have been influenced by the academic and clinical work on the use of interpreters with deaf clients in mental health contexts (Frishberg 1990, Harvey 1982, 1989, Ingram 1974, Roe and Roe 1991, Stansfield 1981). Deaf clients are a truly silent and unacknowledged minority who have for some time been served in clinical contexts with the use of interpreters who translate American Sign Language into verbal language for the clinician. Review of the literature in this arena proves absolutely pertinent for verbal language translators as well. It is rather striking that, in this domain, the thinking, procedures, and experiential acumen of the field of communicative disorders have never been recognized in the formal mental-health literature.

Suggested Guidelines

Guideline 1

Meet with the translator in a brief pre-session consultation so that you can assess their level of competence and appropriateness as a translator in a mental-health context. Review ethical standards with them, stressing confidentiality, and the commitment to render a faithful translation and not interject personal opinions into the client's narrative (Glasser 1983, MacKinnon and Michels 1971, Roe and Roe 1991). If they are not trained, describe the process of *concurrent translation* to them, and tell them that you are seeking word-for-word narratives, and not their summaries. This process may in fact be hard to achieve for those who are untrained, but should be kept in mind as a goal. Untrained translators are usually more comfortable with *sequential translation*, in which they translate chunks or units of narrative. Emphasize that they are speaking in the *patient's voice* and to maintain use of the first person pronoun "I" (i.e., *direct translation*). Instruct especially inexperienced translators that they will be speaking as if they were the client. I find this to be an extremely influential cue that is not particularly difficult for even inexperienced translators to follow. In addition to being instructed about rendering faithful translation, the translator needs to be told to relay along with the translation an affective tone that matches the client's (Glasser 1983, Sabin 1975).

Guideline 2

Introduce the translator to the client, but clearly state to the client that it is you, the clinician, who will be conducting the interview with them. Emphasize that the translator will behave as a "verbal shadow" for each of you, directly translating and narrating everything that is said verbatim. Explain that the translator will be following the code of confidentiality for everything that transpires in the interview (Roe and Roe 1991).

   In the seating arrangement, seat yourself in closer proximity to the patient than the distance between yourself and the translator, or the translator and the patient. This is to emphasize the primacy of the patient–clinician dyad. The translator should be placed on the side at a further distance. Position and align yourself full-faced and full-bodied with the patient so that you are in close facial view of each other and can clearly pick up on physical, nonverbal cues of communication and contact. Even though you may not speak the patient's language, communicate as much as you can with your physical presence that this is a dyadic interchange. Emphasize maintenance of eye contact with your patient versus the translator, communicating that they—the patient—are your source. In the beginning of the session, ask the patient to avoid "talking to the translator"; tell them to "talk to you." As noted by Bradford and Muñoz (1993) in their use of translators for psychotherapy, "[the] translator's importance is obvious, and remains so, but the prominence of the translator's role [can be] allowed to dissolve into a linguistic medium to allow the therapist and patient to confront one another without unnecessary barriers" (p. 54).

TRAINING MENTAL HEALTH TRANSLATORS

In the following section, I would like to describe the basic elements of a training curriculum for mental-health translators. My perspective has been informed both by the clinical literatures that have emerged from various mental-health disciplines and, as noted above, guidelines established by the field of communicative disorders (Roe and Roe 1991) for use by interpreters for the deaf in mental health contexts. These directives emerge from the fact that American Sign Language has been designated the official language of deaf people in the United States and Canada. The Registry of Interpreters for the Deaf has developed a formidable set of training criteria, ethical standards, and procedural guidelines for the use of American Sign Language interpreters that I think have relevance to the use of verbal bilingual translators in the clinical setting (Harvey 1982, 1989, Roe and Roe 1991, Solow 1981).

Training for mental-health translators should be administered by a proficient bilingual mental-health clinician who is extremely conversant in cross-cultural clinical work. The training consists of didactic information, role playing, and supervised client exposure. This can be done in either an individual or group format. Basic prerequisites for the mental-health translator include balanced verbal proficiency in English and another language, and average intelligence. Actual bilingual competence should be assessed formally, if possible (Price 1975). Preparation of translators should include training in the following areas:

Curriculum Content Areas

1. Establishing Ethical Standards

The cardinal rule of confidentiality must be impressed upon translators. All material verbalized by the client, and proceedings transpiring during a clinical session, must be maintained confidential and never be discussed outside of relevant consultation with the clinician who used the translator's services. From guidelines established for American Sign Language interpreters in mental-health settings also emerge the following requisites (Roe and Roe 1991, Solow 1981): translators should render their translations faithfully and not interject their personal opinions or interpretations of the client's discourse. Also, translators should accept assignments using discretion with regard to the level of skill required and the clients involved. A client who is known to the translator or who evokes personal or subjective reactions in the translator should not be accepted.

2. Information on Mental Processes

A cursory overview should be offered on general psychological functioning and the spectrum of affective, cognitive, and behavioral functions that can be impacted when people are in emotional distress. Clearly, if the translator is already a mental-health professional, this would not be necessary. However, underscoring that the assessment goal is to evaluate the operations or dynamics of the client's own thought processes is relevant for all translators, regardless of their level of clinical sophistication. The clinician is not searching for the succinct articulation of ideas, but rather is interested in how a client's thinking works, with all of its disorganization, potential tangentiality, illogic, and so on. Interpreters need to be told of the natural tendency to "clean up" a patient's narrative, and be reminded to render a word-for-word translation as much as they are able. Price (1975) makes note of translators' difficulties in following extremely psychotic, delusional thinking, in particular.

3. Information on Subjective and Emotional Issues that Are Commonly Evoked in Clinical Settings

Translators need to be informed of what we clinicians designate as *countertransference reactions*. This can be explained fairly easily by simply describing how clients can sometimes arouse personal reactions in mental-health workers. I use examples such as: a passive, depressed older female patient who may remind one of one's own mother, or a patient who arouses one's physical attraction. The process of *identification* can also be described, such as strongly connecting to a patient who has also just separated from a love partner, or to a parent whose rebellious adolescent is similar to one's own child.

Interpreters need to be taught that these subjective reactions can sometimes affect their professional work with clients, sometimes quietly moving (i.e., *unconsciously*) their activities in a certain direction. For the translator, these activities can take the form of either translating the patient's narrative in a more confused or pathological light, or the converse—of underemphasizing the patient's pathology in the translation. Sometimes the simple *identification* with a patient of one's own ethnic group can influence a worker toward underemphasizing conflict and pathology (Freed 1988).

The translator should be told that personal prejudices and agendas must be kept out of the translation work. Opinions in such areas as politics, sexual orientation, abortion rights, and so on, cannot influence their translating functions.

4. Linguistic Aspects of Translation

As noted, I recommend Bradford and Muñoz's (1991) model for translators in the clinical situation. In this model, translation is both *concurrent*, that is, occurring as simultaneously as possible to the client's narrative, and *direct*, that is, a literal word-for-word translation of the patient's discourse. However, as also noted earlier, I do not favor the use of this or any other translator model for psychotherapy, other than interventions which are of an extremely cognitive, informational, or psychoeducational nature. This model is, however, extremely effective in assessment and diagnostic interviewing situations, and can be taught to balanced bilingual speakers with a degree of guided practice and supervision.

Concurrent translation

Can be easily demonstrated through observation of a translated clinical interview and role playing within the training situation. This is highly recommended. The general gestalt of "self as translator" that needs to be conveyed is that of the translator as a communication facilitator between therapist and client, or mediator of the verbal flow between the therapeutic dyad, who must maintain as unobtrusive a posture as possible in the interaction. This is also the perspective assumed by American Sign Language translators in mental-health contexts (Roe and Roe 1991, Stansfield 1981). This position is something of an ideal, for we know from sociolinguistic analyses of three-way interactions that interpreters do exert subtle but definite vectors of influence in the triad (Roy 1992). I have found concurrent translation narratives in clinical situations to follow three to seven seconds behind the patient's narrative, given the demands of decoding and translation processes, and the proficiency of the translator. During the initial segments of a clinical session, there is usually a "settling in" period in which the client adapts to the simultaneous talk of the translation situation, and the translator accommodates to the pacing and emphatic contours of the client's (and therapist's) speech. This approach clearly differs from the *sequential translation* method favored by others such as Glasser (1983) and Westermeyer (1990), who encourage small units of information to be translated, where the patient speaks and pauses, then is followed by the translator's narrations of the unit. There are pitfalls to this approach, for it encourages the facile tendency of the translator to "summarize" the units of information, thus encouraging both meaning interpretation and the subjectively selected exclusion of information. Bradford and Muñoz (1993) also note the potential operation of the recency effect in sequential translation, where translators may tend to recall the last pieces of data in a narrative segment better than they recall the middle or initial segments. Concurrent translation can be demanding and fatiguing to the translator, and should include rest-breaks when necessary. This translation approach is demanding, and in the training situation will require significant practice.

Literal or direct translation

Is another element of this model. This is word-for-word translation of the client's utterances. This approach is especially important in the assessment of cognitive processes in a mental status exam, as it permits the clinician to observe the organization and flow of ideas as directly as possible. The approach thus also exerts some control on the translator's tendency to "clean up" a client's discourse and make it more understandable. Also, given the cross-cultural nature of the therapeutic dyad, *direct translation* highlights aspects of the client's use of symbols and meanings that may be foreign to the clinician and thus permits further clarifying inquiry. Even given the translator's knowledge of the cultural context of the client, I favor that the burden of "cultural clarification" of a word meaning, idiomatic reference, or culture-specific behavior be on the therapeutic dyad instead of the burden of "cultural clarification" being on the translator. This is a position currently favored in cross-cultural clinical work, which has invigorating and productive influences on the clinical dyad (Ibrahim 1985, Pérez Foster 1993b, Tyler et al. 1985).

My impression from reviewing the literature on the use of

translators in the clinical situation is that the translator model
which emphasizes the role of the translator as a "cultural interpreter" who can be on-the-ready to explain the cultural meanings and contexts of the patient's narratives is, in fact, driven by
the clinician's own anxiety and vulnerability upon being in the
presence of an ethnic stranger (Pérez Foster 1998). I believe that
there has been an overemphasized rush to solicit assistance from
the ethnic translator, and that this rush emerges from the
clinician's cultural countertransference (see Chapter 9). The
emphasis seems to be on the clinician keeping "hands off"
the struggle to understand and personally grapple with the ethnic stranger. Has this been a very subtle form of racism? As noted
by Stansfield (1981) and Roe and Roe (1991) in their articulation of guidelines for the use of American Sign Language translators with deaf clients, there are times when a clarification or
brief post-session discussion may be necessary between translator and clinician. This may certainly be of help in the cross-cultural clinical situation under discussion here. However, as noted
by these authors, the respective roles of clinician and translator
are clearly defined so that the responsibility is on the clinician
alone to ultimately interpret and guide intervention. In addition,
the fact that a brief discussion of this sort has taken place (or
may take place) is always communicated to the client.

Bradford and Muñoz (1993) highlight the point that, inherent in the *direct translation* approach is, by definition, the
translator's use of the pronoun "I"—or speaking directly in the
client's voice. I emphasize this latter point to translators, underscoring that they are the direct voice of the client to the clinician, and find it to be an extremely influential cue.

Affective translation

Mere translation of words without their accompanying feeling is
not desirable. The translator's voice and expression should reflect the affective tone of each interchange (MacKinnon and
Michels 1971) without, however, mimicking the patient to such

an exaggerated degree that it becomes an awkward parody and distraction to the work (Bradford and Muñoz 1993). Sabin (1975) has highlighted the dangers of overemphasizing the cognitive elements of clinical translation and not focusing enough attention on the affective and subjective aspects of the patient's narratives. He aptly titles his 1975 paper "Translating Despair."

In summary, the spectrum of guidelines that I have delineated in this chapter for the training of mental health-translators can be easily offered didactically in a one-to-one or group format. However, Item 4, which involves the actual linguistic aspects of interpretation, should be offered with active role-playing, observation, and initial practice under supervision. Videotaping could also be very helpful for studying discrete elements of the translation process.

PART III

TREATING THE
BILINGUAL PERSON

Part III deals with the treatment of bilingual people in the clinical setting. It will be of particular help to clinicians who treat clients in their second language, and who have no familiarity with the client's mother tongue. I can very much empathize with the reader of this volume who now, hopefully convinced of the power of language in the psyche, has become concerned enough to ask: So what do we do? Is there any segue to the world of the patient's native language meaning for the clinician who cannot speak its words?

Upon my own first readings and understanding of the cross-disciplinary bilingualism literature, I frankly began to feel rather anxious about the fair amount of work I was doing with patients who were for example primary Russian, Chinese, Italian, or Turkish speakers. I speak none of these languages. How much material was I missing? Was I conducting a "pseudotherapy" with them? Was the clinical work in English simply an enactment of their defensive resistance—that is, of their ability to use the second language to isolate and split off deep emotional material lived in the native language? Aside from considering the literature, I began to do two things: first, to present my work and to organize panels with fellow bilingual clinicians who, as I did, tended to work with a variety of polyglot patients—thus creating a forum for exchanging ideas and interventions. And secondly, I also began simply to ask my bilingual patients for help in entering their native language worlds. I thank them all for what they taught me. In most cases what they offered me in the course of our work together went far beyond cognitive instruction and on to new levels of meaningful intersubjective contact with them. My own vulnerability and confusion, and patients' variable responses to that, permitted new facets of the transference–countertransference to emerge as active working material for work in the therapeutic field.

In Chapter 9 I will first step back from the specificity of linguistic issues as such, and into the wider arena of general countertransference reactions of therapists working in cross-cultural therapeutic dyads. I discuss the multiple subjective facets of experience that commonly engage therapists in their work with bicultural and bilingual people. Chapters 10 and 11 offer an array of case material from both clinical and supervisory settings, and delineate the use of numerous interventions for use by the clinician. In Chapter 11, these interventions emerge from a review of conceptual perspectives on language and bilingual phenomena. Chapter 12 is designed for the clinician as a condensed guide for specific clinical contexts, and is keyed to the text.

9

The Clinician's Cultural
Countertransference

In order to open Part III, the treatment section of this volume, I think it worthwhile to step back from the language factors that influence work with bilingual people, and address the broader panorama in which our treatment with bilingual patients takes place. Similar to the *assessment* of bilingual patients (Chapter 6), so does their clinical *treatment* fall within the larger scope of complex dynamics that are inherent to cross-cultural interactions. In fact, the work done in cross-cultural therapeutic dyads has been brought to task of late for its multiple difficulties in adequately addressing the needs of ethnic clients. In the cross-cultural therapeutic dyad, we are working with clients whose worldviews, life goals, and symptomatic expression may differ from those of the clinician, or the canon of Western-oriented mental health theories and practices. While I have focused on and emphasized the clinician's need to understand the dimensions of native language for the proper assessment and treatment of immigrant clients in this volume, it is important to emphasize in this chapter the comprehensive context of other theoretical, clinical, and personal idiosyncratic issues within which the clinician's work with bilingual clients is embedded.

One might say that, at this time, clinical practice with clients whose ethnicity, race, or class renders them minority groups in American society is undergoing a crisis. The multidisciplinary mental-health field as a whole has come to the disturbing realization that therapeutic services for ethnically diverse groups lack competent effectiveness (Abramowitz and Murray 1983, Atkinson 1985, Sue 1988, Sue and Sue 1990). Criticisms highlight discriminatory practices directed toward ethnic groups, therapists' poor understanding of the cultural contexts of their ethnic clients' lives, and the basic inaccessibility of adequate services available to immigrant populations (Sue 1988, Sue and Sue 1990). In addition, questions have been raised in the clinical literature about the value of even using insight-oriented therapies with minority patients. Usually this recommendation is made in the context of recognizing immigrant clients' practical needs for concrete services. However, notwithstanding this fact, I also believe that this recommendation emerges from a dangerous bias within our field: that people from racial minority and immigrant groups lack the capacity for self-reflection and are unable to explore the meaning of their experiences (Olarte and Lenz 1984, Pérez Foster 1993).

Clinicians are well aware that their client populations now span a diverse range of ethnic and socioeconomic groups. However, they are not so willing to meaningfully address the fact that this new diversity begins to challenge the generalizability of clinical assumptions and practice methods beyond the original European and American populations for which they were designed. Thus, do we question the treatment capacity of ethnic people or question the efficacy of the treatment practices themselves, when faced with the rather disturbing (but also not surprising) data that ethnic minority groups are the least frequent users of mental health services? In addition, when these groups do utilize these services, they show the highest premature termination rate of any social group (Sue 1988, Sue and Sue 1990). Something is clearly amiss here!

In the admitted attempt to grapple with these disturbing findings, the mental-health literature of the last decade has been attempting to address the formidable criticisms that have been leveled on the ethnocentric value presuppositions which inform many theories of normative human development and abnormal psychology (Cirillo and Wapner 1986). In the clinical arena, these

assumptions directly inform diagnostic criteria, treatment interventions, and therapeutic goals. These phenomena have been
articulated in the recent works of Altman (1993), Kirschner
(1990), Ibrahim (1985), Pérez Foster (1996a,b), Guernaccia and
colleagues (1996), LaBruzza and Mendez-Villarrubia (1994), and
others.

In this chapter, however, I would like to take a more
psychodynamic approach to exploring how cultural biases influence the clinician's practice lens in work with ethnic clients, and
highlight the role of what I have termed the *clinician's cultural
countertransference*.[8] The contributing role of the clinician's own
subjectivity in the practice arena cannot be more vital than in
the work clinicians do with patients whose culture, race, or class
differs from their own. Contemporary psychoanalytic observations
of therapeutic interaction point out in no uncertain terms that
the psychotherapeutic frame cannot hide either the clinician's
own worldview, or the many facets of the clinician's own subjective inner self (Aron 1990, Greenberg 1991, Hoffman 1983,
1991). The myriad subjective reactions that are aroused in the
socio-ethnic unmatched dyad are particularly charged with and
embedded within the resonating and reverberating influences of
the socio-environmental milieu. Notwithstanding the acknowledged power of the patient's transferential projections onto the
therapist, what I am speaking of here are the therapist's own feelings of, for example, sadness, despondency, or guilt about the
client's life circumstances; or therapist reactions that might span
the range of confusion, fear, or prejudice toward an ethnic
stranger. It is disturbing to consider, but these reactions are all
potentially discernible to our clients. At the very least, a client's
quiet realization of our unspoken and forbidden attitudes will
create formidable impasses in the work. At worst, as I have stated
in earlier publications, these realizations can lead to premature
termination (Pérez Foster 1993b, 1996a). In my view, these silent recognitions made by ethnic clients about our attitudes, are

---

8. This concept first appeared in Pérez Foster 1998.

manifested in the high premature dropout rate recorded by Sue (1988) and others. Clients from oppressed groups or whose cultural values command respect for the elder will not confront the therapist with their observations; they will simply never return to treatment!

It is the position of several recent writers that, even for clinicians who may have committed their work to service with diverse groups, the choppy waters of cross-cultural, cross-race, and cross-class clinical interaction are often fraught with anxiety and evoke a sense of vulnerability in the therapist (Altman 1993, Gorkin 1996, Mays 1985, Thompson 1989, 1996). I call this subjective state within the therapist the *clinician's cultural countertransference*. Consisting of both cognitive and affective factors, the clinician's cultural countertransference includes a complex and interacting set of culturally based life values, academically based theoretical beliefs and clinical practices, emotionally charged biases about ethnic groups, and biases about the clinician's own ethnic self-identity. Within the full spectrum of subjective characterological issues that all therapists bring to their clinical work, these elements represent the therapist's own particular culture-driven countertransferential set, if you will, one which can consciously and unconsciously be communicated to clients at many levels of interpersonal and intersubjective contact. Like any other fairly dissociated transference phenomena, this state in the therapist holds significant potential for enactment within the treatment, and can maintain such traction as to create impasses in the work that are as powerful and derailing as any impasses produced by the client.

Traditionally, in the psychodynamic therapeutic method, attention has focused on the transferential movements of the client. However, the contemporary psychoanalytic literature on clinical technique has developed a significant volume of work on the contributing role of the therapist's countertransference in the therapeutic process. Originally seen as a neutral participant in the therapeutic encounter, the clinician was also idealized as an unconflicted and optimally healthy figure. Racker (1968) pointed out that this view led to the idea that it was only the patient who developed transferences. Furthermore, the therapist was designated as the supposed optimal representative of "objective reality"; it was the patient who was driven by a sometimes distorted, inner-generated "psychic reality" (Aron 1991). Traditionally, transference developments of any sort in the therapist were viewed as undesirable and hopefully infrequent lapses. However, the important contemporary works of Racker (1988), Hoffman (1983, 1991), Aron (1990, 1991), Gill (1983), Wolstein (1988), and Greenberg (1991a,b) have pulled clinicians out from behind the contrived and unrealistic screen of therapeutic neutrality, and into a light which shows that the therapeutic enterprise is an interaction between the subjectivities of two formidable personalities in the room, each of whom is influenced by the exigencies of their inner and external worlds.

The contemporary clinical literature has catapulted us forward and offered us a more balanced consideration of how the therapist's envy, competitiveness, erotic feelings, and anger can influence the therapeutic work (Greenberg 1991, Wolstein 1988). However, the psychodynamic literature has not yet fully explored the clinical influence of the therapist's ethnocultural and racial identifications and assumptions. While it may be difficult to acknowledge, we bring into our consulting rooms our formidable personalities, and we hold significant prejudices about what kinds of people are more desirable than others; what defines appropriate, healthy behavior; and what endeavors best express the meaning of our cultural life view. We do not differ from our clients here, each of us being immersed in the invisible ethnocentric oxygen of our cultures. While on an intellectual level many clinicians have pursued the zeitgeist of education in cultural diversity, I frankly do not believe that we have permitted ourselves full awareness of how deeply our biases influence our treatment interactions. These biases are embedded in both the basic theoretical and technical approaches to our work, and the deep personal fantasies that we hold about ethnic groups—including our own.

THE COGNITIVE AND AFFECTIVE FACETS OF THE CLINICIAN'S CULTURAL COUNTERTRANSFERENCE

My clinical work in New York City, with an extremely divergent population of immigrant clients, has never ceased to challenge the traditional premises of my clinical training, nor allowed me to deny the fear-based assumptions that I form about people who are different from myself. My professional life has also given me the opportunity to educate and supervise psychology, social work, and psychiatric clinicians who, in the early stages of their clinical work, are just beginning to discover the complex power of their reactions when in the presence of an ethnic stranger. These observations are both disturbing and heartening, for they put shameful feelings on a common plane and give us hope that by acknowledging their presence in all of us, we clinicians can also begin to work them through.

From these experiences I formed the notion of the clinician's cultural countertransference, viewing it as a subjective composite of culture-relevant cognitive and affective factors that influence our clinical work with clients (Pérez Foster 1993b, 1996c, 1998). In a current publication I describe the cultural countertransference as a complex "matrix of four intersecting pools of cognitive and affect-laden experiences/beliefs that exist at varying levels of consciousness within the therapist" (1998, in press). These interacting areas of knowledge and subjective experience include the therapist's (1) American life values system, (2) academically informed theoretical beliefs and practice orientation, (3) personally driven idealizations and prejudices toward ethnic groups, and (4) personally driven biases about his or her own ethnicity. I would like to describe each of these separately.

American Life Values

The emergent interaction among the fields of anthropology, psycholinguistics, and developmental psychology has clearly described the way primary caretakers interpret and teach a culture's meaning system to their children (Harwood et al. 1996, Schweder 1991, Stigler et al. 1990). This information is finally reaching clinicians who are now beginning to understand that culture groups—and their direct messengers, the child caretakers—establish unique parameters about such human functions as self-definition, self–other separation, intersubjective attunement, permeability of outer ego boundaries, and the titration of impulse and emotional expression (LeVine 1990, Roland 1988, 1996). "Cultures shape the understanding of one's self-place in the world, as well as define the thresholds and boundaries of connection and communication with others" (Pérez Foster 1998, p. 257).

American clinicians are educated about mental health and mental pathology within a culture that maintains a very particular view of the self. The traditional American view of humanity is based on Anglo-American religious and secular values that hold the notion of individual responsibility in high esteem. Thus American caretakers tend to teach their children to prize autonomy of the self above all human attributes (Cushman 1991, Kirschner 1990). The psychodevelopmental theories developed by British and American theorists in fact maintain that this self develops from deep dependency with another to ultimate individuated autonomy. As clinicians we are part of a cultural ethic that measures the pathology of this self by its ability to negotiate the wish for merger with the desire to stand alone (Pérez Foster 1996c). We are so immersed as clinicians in our own ethnocentric oxygen, so to speak, that we hardly stop to question whether this image of being a self is at the heart of all people. However, when we are confronted with treating an ethnic stranger, our initial anxiety and puzzlement about them can sometimes turn to the realization that our concept of the human self is by no means universal, but circumscribed by our own unique view of how to be human in the American world. For example, there are devoutly religious Caribbean women who view their lives not as a self-propelled course, but as a painful reenactment of the life of Mary, the mother of Jesus (Gil and Vazquez

1996). There are Asian groups dominated by Hindu and Buddhist beliefs who strive not for individuated autonomy, but for ultimate merging with the cosmos (Roland 1988). And some Pacific Island groups (Lesser 1996), do not see themselves as individual and distinct entities, but as integral pieces in a predestined life scheme in which they play a prescribed role.

Contrary to our assumptions, the American notion of the individually directed and highly autonomous individual represents a unique view of being human that is not held by the majority of world cultures (Cushman 1995, Roland 1988, 1996, Sampson 1988). Many non-Western culture groups have a sense of personhood that is of an "ensembled" rather than a unique self nature (Sampson 1988). The self is viewed as comprising of a matrix of familial, individual, spiritual, and social hierarchical identifications. Children are taught that their feelings and behavior are deeply linked to internalized ancestral influences and spiritual traditions. These points are just beginning to be understood by our Western clinical tradition, which has constructed a description of behavioral phenomenology and diagnostic criteria for its assessments that is narrowly and ethnocentrically based on selfhood within American life (LaBruzza and Mendez-Villarrubia 1994). Clinicians must become conscious of the fact that they carry their American-life value system into their work with clients. These American folkways have become integrated into the American mental health field's constructed definitions of ego functioning and the criteria that distinguish psychic health from psychopathology. These beliefs thus constitute one of the important disavowed elements of the clinician's cultural countertransference.

Academically Informed Theoretical Beliefs and Practice Orientation

Adding to the clinician's cultural value system and view of healthy adaptive living in the American milieu, are the clinician's educationally informed theoretical and metapsychological beliefs about what drives the human condition. Within the sphere of psychodynamically oriented views of psychopathology, clinicians all manage to agree on the presence of the unconscious, and its determined role in the expression of psychic distress (Wolstein 1992). However, clinicians often wed themselves to those metapsychological constructs most consistent with their own view of what drives the human condition. Thus the "instinct story" (Freud 1905), the "object relations story" (Fairbairn 1952, Winnicott 1965), the "will story" (Rank 1945) and the "self story" (Kohut 1971), to name only the most popular metapsychologies, constitute the spectrum of viewpoints that are animatedly debated and elaborated in the psychodynamic clinical literature. However, not until recently have these constructs been considered in the context of their ethnopsychological origins (Pérez Foster et al. 1996).

> It is sobering to consider the observations of contemporary social scientists such as Schweder (1991), Kirschner (1990), Stigler, Schweder and Herdt (1990), and Bruner (1986), who point out that psychological theories that carry the strongest power are those which rationalize and extend a group's most deeply rooted and dearly held traditions and beliefs. Is it a surprise that out of a Victorian society so preoccupied with the harnessing of desire there emerged a psychology of human instincts and a guide-map for how people negotiate between their passions and their inhibitions (Freud 1905)? Is it a surprise that in America, the land of opportunity, upward mobility, and self-actualization, there flourished an ego psychology movement which attempted to define and quantify conflict-free action in the world (Bellak 1948, Goldstein 1995, Hartmann 1964)? And the current zeitgeist, the object relations movement transported from Britain (Fairbairn 1952, Guntrip 1968, Winnicott 1965), thrives in this country because of the theory's very syntonicity with the American way (Greenberg and Mitchell 1983, Skolnick and Warshaw 1992). Resting on the same philosophical bedrock of individualism, these two cultures, the American and the British, are very preoccupied with questions about balancing

the need for meaningful connection with the need for individuated autonomy.

We clinicians are now being informed that theories which inform our clinical work basically elaborate and formalize a group's implicit views on how to function within *it* as desirable and capable human beings (Bruner 1986, Cirillo and Wapner 1986). And therapists move toward those theoretical beliefs which resonate, validate, and express their own life view. Furthermore, these theoretical meaning systems provide both the diagnostic and clinical lenses through which we orient our practice approaches. [Pérez Foster 1998, pp. 258–259]*

The following are some clinical situations that bring a few of our clinical theoretical assumptions into question:

- How do we understand the deep experience of self within a Middle Eastern man from a religious caste, who feels that without the tribe he was trained to lead, his self-esteem is nonexistent, unformed? Do we view him through the American lens of self psychology as a narcissistically derailed self? The ego-psychological lens of a poorly differentiated self? Or, as a person centered in the ensembled self experience of his Eastern culture, where affiliation and group kinship produce individuals who are deeply identified with others throughout life (Pérez Foster 1996c, 1998, Roland 1988)?
- How can we comprehend the psychic world of a Japanese woman who silently waits for the clinician to intuit all of her inner experiences? Some might interpret her stance in Kleinian terms, placing her on a spectrum of paranoid-schizoid/depressive positions. However, the clinician might also come to understand that for this woman, whose culture has trained her in fine nonverbal attune-

---

*This segment first appeared in *Clinical Social Work Journal,* vol. 26, copyright © 1998 by Human Sciences Press, and is reprinted by permission.

ments, most meaningful connection will occur at these nonverbal points of intersubjective communication. [Doi 1962, Pérez Foster 1996c, 1998]

Trying to face the difficult theoretical questions posed by these clients crystallizes the automaticity with which, I think, we use our theoretical formulations. We tend to parse, condense, and interpret large spectra of human behavior into the meaning systems constructed by our respective metapsychological formulations. And each of these formulations highlights behaviors and dynamics that have particular meanings within certain cultural groups. I underscore the automaticity of these theoretically driven interpretive activities to emphasize their disavowed determinism, and thus their role in the clinician's culturally determined countertransferential set.

The Clinician's Personally Driven Biases toward Ethnic Groups

This countertransferential issue now broaches the more deeply subjective and affectively driven culture-related issues that every clinician brings into their work. These are the deep prejudices of our own experience, that our clinical training and clinical treatment can often not dispel (if they are ever broached at all). My own view is that clinical training in ethnic diversity is helpful, but ineffectual unless also accompanied by some experiential and emotional working through of one's biases and fears of others. An interesting observation made by Gorkin (1996) is that even supposedly open-minded clinicians can hide their deep prejudices by making themselves appear as if they are "special cases" who bear no biases. This message can be silently conveyed to clients who begin to collude with the therapist, thus creating "an island" (p. 163) of the treatment situation. This collusion between therapist and patient makes the dyad an ideal or special case in which bias and prejudice do not exist. Gorkin notes that this type of silent collusion can render discussion of cultural differences off limits to the treatment, and beyond the pale of exploration. The danger here of course is that the disavowed is so often unconsciously enacted. Some hidden and forbidden agendas within the therapist might include:

- If I treat a black man in psychotherapy, maybe I'll become less afraid of black men.
- If I do clinical work with the poor and uneducated, they won't notice that I'm in fact not a particularly competent clinician.
- If I treat a client from ethnic group X, maybe I'll discover that they are not so cold, unintelligent, greedy, unemotional, and so on.

In my experience, in matters of forbidden cultural and racial feelings, conscious behavior eventually fails to hide deeper negative and anxiety-driven attitudes toward others, and these become manifest to the client. These attitudes can be so deeply grooved as to be evoked simply by the cadence of intonation or awkward grammar of an ethnic client who presents for treatment with heavily accented English. The evocation of cognitive or affective attitude states can occur through the sensorial dimension of language per se, thus creating a particular form of the cultural countertransference in the clinician which I would label as a *linguistic countertransference*.

The Clinician's Personally Driven Biases about His/Her Own Ethnicity

Submerged within therapists' deeply personal cultural prejudices and idealizations are their attitudes about their own ethnicity. These are feelings about their own Jewishness, sexual orientation, color, Asian origins, lower-class background, and so on. These silent attitudes can also find their way into the therapeutic field. I emphasize here the situation in which it is the clinician's cultural group that has been socially or historically oppressed by the patient's group. This particular dyad has not been sufficiently acknowledged for the potential power of its mutual transferential interaction. Examples of these dyads are when Hispanic therapists treat Anglo clients, when homosexuals treat heterosexuals, when Irish treat English, when blacks treat whites, when Jews treat Anglo-Saxons, or when working-class therapists treat middle-class clients.

Therapists need to remain vigilant of this potential transference to the patient, and mindful of not using the clinical situation to enact culture-laden personal conflicts. This would include a wide range of possibilities such as, for example, finally exercising one's own power over the "aggressor" or, conversely, becoming inhibited by him. I have not infrequently seen the latter situation in young clinicians of color who treat white patients. Their hesitancy in making interpretations of the client's narrative can often be a form of "keeping their place" with the white person in power. I would further add that the tendency of clinicians of color to treat their own ethnic group is often a multidetermined enterprise. On the manifest level these determinants include the desire to help one's community, and one's membership in social and community networks that would tend to make referrals or offer employment situations. On the more latent level could be the belief that one would not be accepted as a competent professional within the dominant white, heterosexual world. These are powerful enactments that, needless to say, need supervisory direction.

The phenomenon that I have described as the *clinician's cultural countertransference* is an interactive set of culturally related cognitions and subjective experiences within the therapist that can exert a mutative impact on the therapeutic process. The cross-cultural, cross-race, and cross-class therapeutic dyad is full of attendant anxieties, fears, insecurities, and questions. Thus far, our focus has concentrated on the patient's anxieties. However, as we move forward with the increased use of contemporary psychodynamic approaches to the clinical process, the therapist's beliefs, biases, and subjectivities are being reconsidered as extremely influential vectors in the therapeutic work, and key influences in the patient's real (vs. transferential) experience of the therapist.

On the cognitive countertransferential plane, our theoretical metapsychology is heavily burdened by its ethnocentrism. These are the academic meaning systems that we use to evaluate healthy living and productive lives. Our theories form the intellectual apex of our cultural countertransference. Together with our American life values, they form as much a part of our culture-bound clinical selves as do our more heartfelt prejudices. On the affective countertransferential plane, whatever therapists fear, desire, or dislike about their client's ethnicity, or whatever therapists degrade or value about their own ethnic group will probably make its way into the action of the therapeutic field.

TOWARD CO-CONSTRUCTION

While recommending approaches for the exploration of transferential phenomena in the cross-cultural dyad is beyond the scope and theme of this book, I would like to offer some broad perspectives which have begun to guide my own work and which I have elaborated elsewhere (Pérez Foster 1993b, 1996c, 1998).

I recognize the presence of Western indigenous beliefs in clinical theory, while also recognizing the wide diversities in human experience and co-experience. But we are left with the problem of how to use the psychodynamic approach with an ever-growing population of diverse patients. In the past we have instituted certain "parameters" in the clinical work, such as offering a second-tier form of real treatment, or no insight-oriented treatment at all (Rendon 1996). Is it our clients who are unworkable or is it our method? Or does our critical self-examination move us toward more valiant shifts in the way we think about human nature and apply our techniques? In this process we would have to become less positivistic in the way that we understand human behavior and more open to formulating meaning through active and reciprocal interactions with our clients—especially when their worlds are so markedly different from our own. This would require clinicians not only to question the ethnocentric assumptions in their understanding of human behavior, but also probably to divulge their vulnerability to a client when they are mystified by aspects of their interaction.

I believe that the clinical literature of the last decade offers us much hope and technical assistance for work in the cross-cultural dyad. For example, what is generally being termed the "narrative turn" in recent clinical treatment (Spence 1982) is introducing a much more balanced and reciprocal view of the treatment process. This perspective views therapy as a meaningful process of co-construction of the patient's life where both members of the dyad are equally involved in the enterprise. The shift is away from the presumptuous primacy placed on the clinician's interpretations, and toward the idea of a joint activity in which two people are focused on creating a coherent life story and understanding what will produce the client's desired change. The recent works of Aron (1991), Greenberg (1991a,b), Saari (1988), Hoffman (1991), Bouchard and Guerette (1991), and others point to the treatment enterprise as a dialectical discourse in which meaning is elaborated by the therapeutic dyad, as well as impacted by each member's inner psychology and view of the world. In this type of therapeutic context, it now becomes incumbent upon clinicians to face the limitations of their own worldview and psychological belief systems, and to bravely move toward truly receiving knowledge from the client. The client, in this respect, is usually far more advanced than the clinician, and has usually already made his or her willingness to be moved by the therapist abundantly clear at the outset of treatment. Moments or episodes of collaboration that I have found particularly meaningful are those where I am conducting a treatment in English—the client's second language—and become aware that there is so much more explanatory detail and affective resonance that lies within the native language. I often ask the client to speak in their tongue, and then translate it to me. I have found that this exchange usually moves far beyond literal translation and instruction, into new domains of contact and connection that is extremely fruitful for the work (see the case of Boris in Chapter 10).

The last decade has also seen the development of what can be generally termed the "culturally competent services literature." From Paniagua (1994), Woody (1991), and Bush and Sainz (1997), for example, emerge methods the practitioner may find useful to explore their own internal value sets, and consider how these may be in conflict with those of the client seeking help. Tyler et al. (1985), LaBruzza and Mendez-Villarrubia (1994), and others have delineated guidelines for understanding both the divergent patterns of well-being and the varied patterns of psychological discomfort that exist among diverse ethnic groups. A basic premise in the thinking of these writers is that empathy and positive rapport are important but singly inadequate elements to carry the cross-cultural dyad through the workings of the therapeutic process. While there may exist some universals in human meaning systems and in the spectrum of affective expression across cultural groups, social scientists have also repeatedly elucidated that there exist complex varieties of meanings connected to human experiences that are culturally distinct and unique (Kitayama and Markus 1994, Lutz 1988). And these must be learned by the therapist.

I take the position that the more disparate the cultural worlds of the therapeutic dyad, the more that the therapeutic enterprise needs to be undertaken as a joint quest for understanding and meaning, with the therapist needing to be particularly cautious about exercising his or her culturally circumscribed view of human behavior. Notwithstanding their sensitivity to the patient's anxieties, clinicians in the cross-cultural dyad must also be keen to the arousals, anxieties, and biases that are likely to occur in *them* upon being in the presence of an ethnic stranger. This view forms the base of my argument that both the cognitive and affective elements of the clinician's cultural countertransference matrix can create vectors in the therapeutic process that are as potent as those forces produced by the patient.

10

Bilingualism in the Clinical Setting: Cases from Practice and Supervision

In the first section of this chapter I would like to use detailed case descriptions to illustrate the roles of bilingualism and culture as dynamic forces in the organization of psychic processes and the expression of psychic distress. I also want to graphically display how these operations become manifest in the clinical setting. I have chosen these particular cases because they highlight the array of psychodynamics that can be influenced by dual-language ability. The cases of Boris and Josefa portray how children can bind, cushion, and transform their inner fears through a language that belongs to a different cultural world. The case of Nina startles the reader to attend to the trenchant power of language in ego operations, to its ability to titrate and forestall psychic disintegration, and to its potential role in diagnostic assessment. Josefa's narrative will remind the reader of the multiply layered significations of word meanings, and the mutative influence of cognitive development on concept formation. And finally, Boris's language-related clinical processes describe the exciting forays into intersubjective connection that can be made by a therapeutic dyad as it shares the sonorous strands of cross-cultural interactive discourse.

The next section of the chapter will open discussion of some heretofore uncharted territory: the impact of the therapist's own bilingualism in the clinical work. It will expand on a process that I noted in Chapter 9 and called the clinician's *linguistic countertransference*, this time exploring the bilingual therapist's own subjective evocations upon using their respective languages. These language-related countertransferential processes will be examined through their reverberation in the clinical work and parallel enactment in the bilingual supervisory setting where clinical supervisee and supervisor share the same language abilities.

THE IMPACT OF LANGUAGE IN THE CLINICAL SITUATION

Boris

A Russian colleague referred to me a fellow countryman who was seeking psychological consultation and treatment. For unclear reasons, the clinician had to fill the requirements of being neither Russian nor Jewish. My Hispanic-American origins and early education in Catholic schools apparently satisfied these criteria, factors that would prove to hold dynamic significance in the subsequent clinical process. Boris was a 47-year-old man who had migrated to the United States from the Ukranian republic of the former USSR in 1991. He was accompanied by his wife, two children, and mother-in-law. After three years of seeking employment, the patient had just recently found a position in his professional area of electrical engineering. He had been working until this time as a night-shift taxi driver. Boris spoke fluent English, a language that he had taught himself as a young man, mostly through reading contraband American literature in his field. He rapidly increased his English proficiency upon arrival in the United States.

At our first meeting, the patient's grave and somber demeanor gave me the impression of a man who was completely consumed by his inner concerns. While cordial in his interpersonal manner, and wanting to make a connection with me, he seemed unable to afford the luxury of a full range of facial or physical expression. Indeed, Boris reported that he had been feeling depressed since his arrival to this country, was currently anxious about his job performance, and felt constricted by acute episodes of dull pain that he experienced in different parts of his body: the stomach and pelvic area, the head, and recently the calves of his legs. A medical workup had indicated no physical findings, and he was referred for psychological evaluation.

On a mental status exam, taken in English, the patient showed no evidence of remarkable cognitive pathology, other than significant somatic preoccupation and the belief that an undiagnosed disease was causing his discomfort. He was generally anxious and his mood was moderately depressed, but he showed no current evidence of compromised behavioral functioning or vegetative signs of an endogenous depression. Inquiry into his Psycholinguistic History (Pérez Foster 1996d) revealed that, for Boris, since boyhood, English had represented the freedom of thought and action that had been so restricted in his native USSR. In addition, the experience of oppression was especially keen for Boris, who had grown up as a Russian-Jewish boy in an anti-Semitic country. Since early childhood he had learned Russian and Yiddish/Hebrew hand in hand, Yiddish for colloquial interaction with family and close ones, and Hebrew for Jewish liturgy and religious life.

As is common with immigrant clients who enter treatment, Boris filled the early months of his sessions recounting the difficult years since his arrival in this country. Gaining passage for himself and family to the United States under the favored immigrant status offered to religiously persecuted Russian Jews, Boris and his wife entered the country with prearranged job commitments and great hopes. Boris's arrangement fell through, however, and he was unemployed for one year before conceding to take a job as a taxi driver. Feeling ashamed, unmanly, and underutilized, Boris marked his depression from this period. He also reported an increasing anxiety around this time about his own and his children's health, whose seeming garden-variety bouts with flu, colds, and viruses are of great concern to him.

After several months of weekly psychotherapy, the patient

appeared somewhat brighter, but still plagued by his physical discomfort. He stated that his conversations in English with me have a "cleansing effect." "English has a way of putting your thoughts in order, without all the Russian that is filled with innuendo." "What innuendo?" I asked. "Well, the 3,000 years of history! I thought I could clear my mind with a person who had no familiarity whatsoever with any of this, and could hear me out free of the mad ideas Russians have!" I thought that Boris was projecting here the clearest signs of someone who was straining in the effort to make sense of obvious inner turmoil through the weakly organized defensive features of a new language. So fragilely constructed and brittle did I assess this defense to be that I decided to allow the surely fulminating pressures of his inner fears to emerge with minimal interpretive help from me.

In the course of his sessions, Boris clarified that his migration to the United States from the Ukraine was in fact circuitous and marked by a violent environmental event in his home state. In 1986, when his children were both infants, the Chernobyl nuclear plant, located approximately fifty miles from his home in the Ukraine, suffered a leakage in one of its reactors, causing an explosion which left the surrounding areas densely contaminated with radioactive fallout. The entire ecosystem was impacted, leading to contamination of food, water, and atmospheric quality. He told me:

> There were large relocations of people to safe-zones; my family was eventually one of them. There was little food and the government was, as usual, secretive about what had really happened. They just told us that we were to be moved for safety. It was like a weird nightmare the days before they moved us. Families who thought they lived in areas that were unaffected would wake to find that their gardens had turned black overnight or that their pets had all died. After a year people died suddenly, sometimes after sudden fevers. There were homes where everyone lost their hair. We ate sparingly, not knowing what was safe. They finally completed our move

to the North. We were in shock, waiting for I don't know
what . . . I resolved to leave my country. I spent three years
trying to get our visas to the United States.

Boris began to share his dreams, which are all in his native
tongues. One day he recounted a dream where a handful of
people from his old town have gathered to pray for all the rest
who have died. In Hebrew he began to recite the mourner's
Kaddish. I recognize it through the sounds of its dolorous cadence. Hearing one of Boris's mother tongues for the first time
I was aware of the complex meaning that its spontaneous introduction will have in our work. Speaking neither Russian nor Hebrew, and somehow not wanting to lose this window into the
patient's deeply felt native world, I responded to him with a few
Spanish lines from a prayer for the dead that is recited in Catholic liturgy in similar cadence. Boris was clearly shaken by the
brusque shift from our orderly English space. Death in Spanish
had come dangerously close to the death in his native emotional
underground.[9]

This dream opened the long course of his inner nightmare:
he, like many other Russian Jews who lived in the Ukraine, harbored the fear that the Chernobyl explosion was not an accident,
but a form of killing Jews once again. His body was contaminated
with radioactivity. So were those of his young children. Death
was coming slowly. This was a Holocaust by radioactivity. Becoming conscious of the dynamic bases of his physical discomforts
served a multiple function. While it began on the one hand to
relieve the belief that he was riddled with disease, the insight
also moved him toward a deeper understanding of the persecu-

---

9. In Chapter 12, I will expand on the use of this intervention from the
perspective of clinical technique and its use by therapists who have no
knowledge of the client's native language.

tory fears that he experienced as a Russian Jewish man who had grown up in an anti-Semitic country. These were fears that he had defensively denied, disparaged as hysterical in others, and refused to admit in himself. A non-Jewish therapist, he believed, would never know about this (and hopefully side with his defensive resistance).

Boris's dreams were often laced with symbols of Jewish liturgy and history—images that he knew I appreciated and understood from my own education and religious self-disclosure. It was also his way of pulling me into the language of his developmental history. His recounting of dreams and fantasies in Russian, then translating them to me in English was an approach we used comfortably, and that served to access the affect-laden memories coded and stored in his original languages. Eventually, Boris was also able to more evenly approach the real medical issues that potentially faced his family as a result of radioactive exposure. He researched the literature and continues to keep abreast of follow-up studies. An international conference convened in Vienna in 1996, "Ten Years After Chernobyl," reporting the results to date of epidemiologic investigations of survivors, in fact documented a higher incidence of thyroid cancers specifically in child survivors of the nuclear accident (Kaul et al. 1996). ·

Boris and I continue to work together, ironically joined by the disparate languages of our respective native beginnings. However, the deep fear of a slow-moving Chernobyl Holocaust still remains—an area of concern for Boris which, when explored in the treatment, will shift our present intersubjective points of contact to potentially terrifying zones of interaction. These explorations will force us to face our disparate ethnic and religious beginnings in a very new way.

Nina

This case illustrates the role of bilingualism in manifest cognitive pathology and the importance of dual language evaluation of mental status.

Nina was a 68-year-old single Venezuelan woman who had migrated to the United States at age 25 with her four adult siblings. She was equally proficient in Spanish and English. She presented at the geriatric psychiatric clinic of a New York hospital for psychiatric evaluation and an assessment of her psychopharmacologic regimen. Nina was referred by an outpatient psychiatric clinic in South Carolina where she had been treated successfully as an outpatient for at least twenty-five years for a diagnosis of chronic paranoid schizophrenia. Nina and her extended family, with whom she had always lived, had just relocated to the New York area and were seeking an outpatient facility to care for her needs.

Psychosocial evaluation of the patient, an interview with family, and review of psychiatric records which were brought in hand revealed a complex and interesting psychiatric history. Nina and her family's original migration to the United States was instigated by political upheaval in Venezuela (and by their involvement in the government). They came to the United States seeking physical safety. Nina was a graduate of a teacher's college in her country and was also a gifted linguist who was fluent in Spanish, English, French, and Italian. In fact, her initial employment in this country was as a multilingual secretary and translator.

Three years after her arrival, Nina suffered her first psychotic break. She was diagnosed with acute schizophrenia, paranoid type, and hospitalized for two years after being found roaming her neighborhood disoriented, floridly delusional, and carrying a kitchen knife in her bag. She was terrified by the belief that indigenous mountain people from her country were following her and wanted to kill her. Nina was treated with the standard clinical intervention for schizophrenia at the time: hydrotherapy, physical restraint, and electroconvulsive therapy. However, in 1955, with the advent of the first antipsychotic medications, Nina was among one of the first cohorts of psychiatric patients in the

United States to be treated with phenothiazines. Nina's primary symptoms abated impressively and she was able to return home with her family, who were supportive and extremely creative in reintegrating her into active functioning. She was given a job in the family business, lived at home, and included in all family social life. Nina's own self-initiated social contacts were minimal, however; she maintained an essentially schizoid posture, and spent most of her free time reading in her room.

Nina was maintained essentially stable for forty years through a combination of antipsychotic medication and functioning in her work and family milieu. During her thirties she experienced some psychotic decompensation; however, these episodes were treated at their onset with pharmacologic readjustment. Monthly evaluation and follow-up of her mental status over the years eventually moved Nina into the chronic schizophrenic designation and, as is noted for some across the life span of this diagnostic group, there was an amelioration over the years of her positive cognitive symptoms for schizophrenia (Cohen 1990). It should be noted that, given Nina's fluency in English, she had always been evaluated and interviewed in this language.

Upon the patient's current presentation at the New York geriatric psychiatric clinic—which is part of a large teaching hospital—available bilingual clinicians astutely proceeded to conduct her interview and mental status evaluation in both English and Spanish—her first language. Strikingly, her English narrative projected cognitive processing that was fairly organized, cohesive, reality oriented, and devoid of autistic or idiosyncratic intrusion. Spanish assessment, however, manifested thinking processes which, while organized, were intruded upon by repetitive themes of a fairly fixed delusional nature. These themes did not emerge in her current English narrative nor were they recorded in her earlier records. This ideation consisted of some of the paranoid beliefs that were prominent during her early psychotic episodes. She in fact still harbored the belief that indigenous people from her country were looking to harm and kill her.

To the best of Nina and her family's knowledge, she had never really received any form of protracted psychotherapy where, within the context of a long-term therapeutic relationship, these beliefs and their associations might have possibly emerged within an albeit English-language interaction. The point is that, during her brief monthly psychiatric follow-ups and during her circumscribed daily functioning at her job, Nina was able to maintain a level of stable cognitive functioning in English that was probably symbolically and affectively removed from the more primitive resonances and associations of her native language. From the review of psychodynamic bilingualism literature, we surmise that this would be the language of her deepest fears, conflicts, and potential psychic disintegration. Indeed, initial superficial exploration of Nina's fears in Spanish by the bilingual clinician suggested that their very personalized meanings had their origins in the patient's early developmental and adolescent history, were associated with the details of the family's unique motivations for leaving their country, and had never really been explored in a therapeutic situation.

When questioned closely about the context and content of her differential language use, Nina divulged that at the end of her workday, her going to her room to "read" was also her special time to talk to herself, think about her concerns, and analyze the "progress" that her persecutors were making in finding her. "I think to myself in Spanish," Nina says. The family confirmed that this sometimes audible "muttering" was always in Spanish, not clearly comprehensible, and something that was always gently reprimanded by "¡Para!" (Stop it!). This was followed by their engaging Nina in some English conversation. Inadvertently, the family had created its own operant conditioning protocol: negatively reinforcing manifest psychotic Spanish verbal behavior, and positively rewarding English verbalizations which were coherent and reality oriented. While these conditions had on the one hand created functional and adaptive behaviors in the English speaking domain (in which the entire extended family mostly lived), they had also reinforced a deep linguistic separation in Nina's psychic life.

The question remains for this 68-year-old woman as to whether some earlier working through and reformulation of Spanish ideation in the context of a psychodynamic engagement with a therapist would have so shifted elements of her psychic structure and internalized object relations as to have promoted some movement of the schizoid posture maintained throughout her relational functioning. I believe that it would have. A more accurate bilingual assessment across the span of her psychiatric treatment could have exposed Nina's more active psychotic thinking in Spanish. This would have probably encouraged formulation of a more comprehensive treatment plan where long-term dynamic treatment might have provided the milieu for some reconstruction of psychic material.

Josefa

I was asked to conduct a Spanish interview and confirm the mental status of a 70-year-old Dominican woman who was an inpatient on the oncology unit of a metropolitan hospital where I was on staff. Hospitalized for a scheduled mastectomy after a breast biopsy revealed a malignancy, the woman was now refusing to sign an informed consent for surgery.

Spanish was Josefa's first language, but she clearly favored speaking in her barely accented English. She was a retired factory worker. She showed no remarkable psychological symptoms when evaluated in either language, other than the circumscribed denial of the malignancy in her breast, which appeared to have presented suddenly upon her hospitalization for surgery. About her present condition she stated emphatically in English, "I don't understand why they want to take away my breast, there's nothing wrong with it. What I probably have is an infection in my chest." She was vague about what this infection might be. Emphasizing repeatedly the distinction between breast and chest, I wondered about what personalized or idiosyncratic meanings she might be ascribing to these terms. Josefa's proper, Old World appearance—embroidered bed jacket and neat bun of white hair—made me think of an elderly señorita, someone who in polite social conversation might consider the term "breast" unseemly, preferring the more demure "chest" instead. I had no time to explore these associations, however, as Josefa agitated for discharge and was released against medical advice. To my surprise, however, she consented to see me in outpatient psychotherapy "to talk things over when I'll be in a calmer state of mind."

I saw Josefa for approximately seven months in weekly treatment. The quality and mood of her English narrative during these sessions was something that I had never quite seen before. Clearly and assertively avoiding the issue of her physical health, she instead launched into an agenda that was very much her own, and had the quality of a rapidly cascading story of her life that had awaited the right time for disclosure. She interacted with me as if I were merely her Wednesday at 3:15 "on" switch. My feeling was that I could have been replaced by anyone who would permit her to speak for forty-five minutes with almost no interruption. She never missed an appointment, was always on time, and punctually paid her bill. I let this unique connection to me evolve, and decided to wait for some cue that would permit me to enter into some semblance of a dialogue with her. I was also extremely aware of Josefa's still-growing malignancy.

Her current and largest life problem, she recounted, was her brother Albert, age 60, an active alcoholic, with whom she had lived all of her adult life. Albert had recently escalated his drinking after a diagnosis of deteriorative liver disease. She was afraid that he was basically killing himself. She made no association here to how she was coping with her own diagnosis; however, I became aware of how Josefa's fear for her brother's health probably paralleled her own anxiety about her unattended malignancy. The siblings had no living relatives, had never married or moved to create separate lives, and had set up home together since Josefa was in her twenties. Josefa described that she had had bad luck with suitors and had always stayed "pure." She finally realized that her destiny was to make a home and care for her younger brother. Chastity and family loyalty, she said with some bitterness, were her finest qualities. While she knew that Albert had affairs with women, and might very well have established his own life apart from her, she knew that he too remained with her out of a deep sense of duty.

In fact, after reviewing these events since Albert's illness, she was beginning to be plagued with guilt for having ruined her brother's life, stood in his way, and railed at him with her bad temper: "In truth, I think I have always resented him—ever since we were children." Josefa conceded to answer a question from me about her early life. She spoke of her girlhood in the Dominican Republic. Naming cities and places in Spanish easily led her to speaking full Spanish, to which I experimentally responded with more active participation. She surprisingly accepted this from me and slowly began to shift her stance to include me in her dialogue. I was relieved. Her family, she said, was loving and kind. When she was 9 however, her brother was born, and the mother left home with a lover, taking the nursing baby with her. Josefa is left with her father and has no memory after the mother's departure, except for the knowledge that the mother soon died. Her first recollection of this period is from age 11, when she is sent along with the now 2-year-old brother to live with two maternal aunts in New York. The father had made the aunts legal guardians of the children. He supported the children financially but rarely visited. Josefa remembered being told by these aunts that their mother died of an infection in her breast or chest. She was not sure which, but the story that she figured in her mind was that "the baby bit my mother's breast when he was feeding and it became infected. I remember thinking that the baby made my mother die, but he didn't know any better, and now someone needed to take care of him." Josefa admitted to having been confused about this story, because other people later told her that her mother had died of tuberculosis—that is, an infection in her chest.

Josefa's confusion about whether her mother suffered a breast or chest infection was likewise present when she used the Spanish words *seno* or *pecho*. Her idiosyncratic association to these words now became clear to me, as did her denial of her own "breast infection." As we moved on in the work, which became both mournful and related, it was clear that Josefa's clarification of her own breast condition had to be prefaced by some working through of her early trauma: the mother's betrayal and death, its relation to her brother, her own abandonment, and the meaning of her current adult life adjustment. With tremendous clarity and insight she said one day: "My brother and I, I think we stay together to not lose our mother again." I saw Josefa in what I thought to be a productive treatment for approximately seven months, at which point she had her surgery. Despite our set plans for her to continue in therapy after her hospitalization, she never returned.

I worked with Josefa early on in my studies on bilingualism. She instructed me in many ways, alerting me to how language use during development can signify and symbolically encapsulate fundamental developmental experiences. I also learned how word meaning, for the developing child, can acquire layers of specialized symbolic meanings that signify the child's evolving levels of cognitive, affective, and psychodynamic development.

Josefa's precise, no-nonsense ("Don't interrupt me"), initial English language narrative, though exaggerated in the midst of her acute distress, reenacted the austerity of her initial English usage with her cold and undemonstrative guardian aunts. At age 11, fresh from her parental abandonment, immigration, and crude immersion into a foreign family, Josefa was heavy-handedly forced to speak English most of the time to accelerate her proficiency. The patient's initial English treatment of me as a replaceable object-thing in the therapy was a projected identification of the feelingless object she was forced to be in the midst of her trauma and in the presence of her aunts. However, when she moved in therapy to the Spanish of her early developmental years, evoking the Spanish era when she was the real feeling child of two loving parents, her transference shifted, allowing us to interact as real human beings.

As portrayed in the cases of Anna and Yulie which I described in Chapter 5, I viewed Josefa's language-evoked transference shifts as projections of language-related self-states. These are developmentally sustained and psychically internalized self–other interactions that are internally represented in the language code through which they were negotiated. As Josefa moved further with her Spanish through the course of treatment, this particular language-related self-state—reenacted within the transference— shifted to other venues and areas of relational developmental experience, in turn evoking further transferential dimensions. I would like to underscore here that I am not proposing the notion of "fixed" language-related transferences, but rather transference phenomena whose dimensions shift and evolve like any others, and that can be evoked in the treatment by shifts in affect state, ideational material, real interactions with the therapist, or language changes in the therapeutic narrative.

Josefa's fascinating play on words for infections of the breast/chest proved to be complexly layered and multidetermined. At ages 9 to 11, with little real explanation from the remaining adults in the world, Josefa's wordplay represented the cognitive attempts of a child trying to make logical sense of an incomprehensible set of events. It was the developmental effort of a latency-age child making use of symbolic language in the service of basic reality-testing. This was an effort which produced no plausible solutions, and rendered the conceptual meanings of the terms confusingly fixed at this cognitive level well into her adulthood. In addition, the semantic confusion was probably also embedded in the word-meaning subtleties of second language acquisition processes, as well as the psychodevelopmental dynamics of a prepubescent girl beginning to cope with her own physical metamorphosis from chest to breast. And at the level of psychodynamic processes, Josefa's play on words represented a defensive solution, that is, a justifiable reason for hating her brother instead of the beloved mother (and father) who had abandoned her. These were the feelings that somehow pressed for consciousness at the time of her surgery. While having devoted her life to making a home for her brother, she also knew that she had tormented him unfairly for "causing" their mother's death.

I would have very much liked to continue work with Josefa. Her resilience and unique solution for survival in the face of her losses moved me. I came to think that her complex defensive forces permitted her to uncover just enough to undergo her surgery, beyond which further analysis would have probably caused her to lose her mother once again.

THE IMPACT OF LANGUAGE IN THE CLINICAL SUPERVISORY SETTING

As an English-Spanish speaking clinician, I have fairly frequent exposure to similarly bilingual mental-health professionals who seek supervision. Given the recency within which native Spanish speaking psychoanalytic supervisors have become available in the North American mental-health field, a common supervisory scenario that I encounter is that of a bilingual supervisee who treats a significant number of Spanish-speaking patients, but who has never had the opportunity to use the actual language of treatment within supervision. Commonly, their cases are supervised by means of translated process recordings with English-speaking supervisors.

Some of these clinicians are trainees from Latin America and Spain who are primary Spanish speakers. However, many of them are, like myself, immigrants to this country or first-generation children of immigrants who possess some balance of bilingualism. I find these latter supervisory situations the most interesting. They often pose fascinating and complex language-related dynamics that involve transferential, countertransferential, and parallel-process phenomena which become manifest in both the treatment and supervisory situation, and have heretofore never been reported in the clinical literature.

THE BILINGUAL CLINICIAN'S LINGUISTIC COUNTERTRANSFERENCE

In Chapter 9, I discussed a phenomenon that I labeled the *clinician's cultural countertransference*. This is a predispositional set of culture-related countertransferential factors that exists within every clinician and which becomes particularly awakened and clinically influential when therapists are faced with a patient whose culture, class, or race differs from their own. I include within this cultural countertransferential set the clinician's cognitively based American life values and academically informed theoretical beliefs, as well as the clinician's more subjectively charged personal biases about ethnic groups. In addition, this subjective countertransference also includes feelings that clinicians harbor about their own ethnicity and the respective power position(s) that their group has held among other ethnic groups. I am proposing here that an additional culture-related countertransferential feature emerges for the bilingual/bicultural clinician. This is the set of deep resonances and associations that is aroused by the clinician's use of each of his or her respective languages in the clinical work.

Following the essential argument of this book, both patient and therapist are bound to hold meaning systems, internalized self–other interactions, and self experiences that are symbolized by each of their respective languages. And paralleling the dynamics of their bilingual patients, bilingual therapists can likewise construct formidable language-related transferences to their patients that can (potentially) exert as much influence on the clinical process as any projections produced by their patients. Given the current clinical trend to throw light on the intersubjective interactions of both members of the dyad in the treatment, the presence of language-related transferential phenomena within the therapist is not something to dismiss.

I have encountered a rich set of language and culture-related dynamics, especially in those Latin American (by birth or descent) clinical supervisees who were raised and educated in the United States. These clinicians are bicultural individuals of varying degrees, as each integrates a unique and personal mixture of North American and Latin American values into their own lives. Externally, these cultural identifications are expressed through variable dual-language use, lifestyle, dress, partner choices, and child-rearing practices. Internally, these cultural identifications are probably deeply etched in varied, multiple, and interactive experiences of self. Upon a supervisee's request I will often conduct the supervision partially or entirely in Spanish because of the Spanish-language clinical treatment that is being discussed. Supervision in the bicultural clinician's developmental language is usually an extremely rewarding enterprise. It can evoke a richer and wider spectrum of countertransferential associations, and pointedly explore the nuances of many language-related intersubjective attunements with the patient that are so often lost in translation. These clinically relevant processes within the clinician, however, are even further compounded and accentuated by the dynamic role that biculturalism plays in their *own* psychic processes.

For many bicultural or bilingual clinicians, the professional self is deeply intertwined with the English language. There are manifest academic reasons for this, as professional training in American schools has rendered them proficient in an English technical lexicon that may not be easily translatable into Spanish. Furthermore, given these clinicians' professional education and working lives in the mainly English-speaking clinical milieu, there is often a de facto context-bound split between their English-speaking professional lives, and the native-speaking life of many of their family and social relationships. And this division

may (or may not) carry itself further into the life of their psychic interior where much internal self-talk, fantasy and dream
life may also be represented in the developmental language. For
these therapists, as is true for their patients, this functional paradigm may in fact reenact a familiar developmental split in which
English evolved as the social language of public intercourse, and
the language through which multiple and complex cognitive
skills were symbolized, while Spanish was maintained as the idiom
of the familial home environment, and the language through
which formative and primary relationships were represented. As
I have argued throughout this volume, for clinicians too the developmental language of primary relationships may be the language within which the full affective and cognitive complements
of their deep narcissistic issues are embedded. One might con-
jecture that the deeper resonances of these issues may have been
circumvented, that is, resisted, in the clinician's English-only psychotherapy or analysis. A bilingual supervision for such a clinician can thus prove to be both a charged and enlightening
enterprise, as it sometimes exposes "language-evoked" impasses
in the clinician's clinical work that are enactments of his or her
own unresolved developmental issues, which may happen to side
very well with patients' current resistance or transference projection of the moment. In supervision, this material can emerge
both in the course of the usual supervisory narrative, or in parallel-process phenomena that reverberate unconsciously in the
supervisory relationship.

A very common occurrence among Spanish-speaking
supervisees, for example, are impasses in the work caused by
their reluctance to confront or interpret material to an older
Spanish client, because of fear that they will offend an elder.
These therapists' initial insight into their countertransferential
behavior is usually interpreted along the lines of Latin-American
social habits and the cultural script of *respeto*, that is, the protocol of deference that a younger person is bound to pay to an
elder in social intercourse. However, despite this awareness, the

impasse may still persist; the therapist may note that this subjectively generated countertransference does not occur in their English-language clinical work, and the language-evoked anxiety may begin to emerge in the process of the bilingual supervisory relationship. These are usually abundant signs that the therapist's behavior goes well beyond "cultural script."

A male, United States–born Latin American supervisee, with years of clinical experience in the area of substance abuse, sought supervision with me for what he experienced as a particularly problematic group of recovering male substance abusers. It was the first time that he had ever conducted a group with men in Spanish, and he imagined that the nuances of language in the group process were possibly escaping him. At the manifest level, linguistic factors were indeed an issue, as the therapist, who was raised in a bilingual home in the United States, was not used to the level of Spanish sophistication in his group of all native-born speakers. The therapist was extremely embarrassed to divulge his occasional lack of comprehension, however, and would instead scurry between sessions to polish his Spanish grammar and vocabulary. At an intersubjective level, his discomfort had nevertheless been clearly communicated to his clients, for at a later phase in the group process, the group members used the therapist's vulnerability in a process of joint resistance. Several members had colluded to subtly depreciate the therapist, and allude to him as a well-meaning but still "wet behind the ears" young man. Linguistic issues notwithstanding, the therapist finally became aware of the traction of his own transference and the power of the Spanish language spoken by men who had recovered from alcohol just like his own father. This was a unique experience for this therapist, distinct from any that he had experienced from his English therapies with male alcoholics. Additionally striking in the supervisory process was the therapist's growing awareness of his pointed switch to English (and avoidance of Spanish) whenever he attempted to explore this impasse in the supervision with me.

Linguistic and cultural issues can sometimes interact within the therapist to create rather complex countertransferential predispositions. I have supervised a number of clinicians whose ethnic or family histories have sculpted their ethnic identifications toward the decidedly more American end of the bicultural spectrum. Thus, first- and second-generation United States–born children of Ukranian, Italian, German, Spanish, Chinese, or Polish parents often hold little conscious memory of the native family language. However, like all disavowed or dissociated segments of the psyche, especially those that are intimately connected to primary object experiences, unconscious early language-related associations often emerge unannounced, segueing through defensive structures and projecting themselves onto the myriad panoramas of everyday human life. As clinicians, our working lives with patients are filled with such projective opportunities. In this way, the American therapist of Italian descent whose family eschewed all traces of their culture for fear of prejudice, secretly revels in the deeply accented English of her Sicilian female client. The client, aware on some level of the role that she is playing in her therapist's subjective interior, dreams one day that they are both sisters. A male therapist, consciously aware of his love for everything Russian and its connection to his mother's Russian heritage, nevertheless finds himself "blindsided, and falling hopelessly in love" with his young Russian patient.

A California-raised Mexican-American clinician whom I supervised several years ago grew up experiencing the forces of institutionalized racism as blocking her full identification as an American. Having been born in the United States, she also did not feel like a true Mexican. In supervision, the therapist became aware that her conducting a long-term treatment with a native-born Mexican woman had served to validate her own ethnicity and reawaken an immersion into her long underused Spanish. An important focus of our supervisory work was to understand the impact of the therapist's countertransference to the patient, and its influence on the therapeutic process. In a supervisory experience that proved to be extremely rich, elements of these complex dynamics were paralleled, enacted, and explored in the supervisory transference, one which had also configured me as a more "ethnically true" Hispanic in both cultural identity and Spanish proficiency.

11

Conceptual Models, Clinical Interventions, and Hope for the Monolingual Clinician

MODELS THAT MOVE CLINICAL INTERVENTION

In this chapter I would like to offer the clinician some helpful interventions for use with clients whose native language they do not speak. These interventions emerge from conceptual models that have been generated by clinical observation and research findings. I would like to first briefly review them.

Psychodynamic Perspectives

Mikhail Bakhtin (1981), a Soviet scholar and literary theorist, maintained a view of the language process that is beginning to be considered within American academic circles, and most recently by some clinicians as well (Amati-Mehler et al. 1993, Harris 1992, Massey 1996). One aspect of his thinking that is of interest to us here is his view of verbal discourse as an activity inhabited by multiple voices, styles, meanings, and enunciations. Embodied within language, he believed, were the memory of human meanings, ideologies, and visions of the world, in all of their historical, stratified, and shifting permutations. While Bakhtin's is considered more of a sociolinguistic than intrapsychic theory of the language process, contemporary psychoanalytic students of language such as Lacan (1977), Stern (1985), and Kristeva (1980), echo the notion of the dense, polymorphous, and multistratified qualities of speech within their particular focus of interest: individual psychic operations. Unlike Bakhtin, who was focused on the creative external products of speech in process, these writers view the variegated dimensions of speech as oral representations of the psychic interior.[10] They see language as the symbolic container of many developmental moments of personal desire, as well as delineating the dynamic characteristics of speech within the individual. With the increasing symbolic elaboration of word meanings throughout a person's development, language comes to serve a complex and sophisticated dual function in a person's life. On the one hand it is a creative and ever-evolving symbolic sculptor for the signification of experience. On the other, it is an intellectualized mechanism for the condensation and distancing of felt experience. Because of this, Lacan (1977) and Kristeva (1989) in particular have contended that language becomes an important mainstay of the psyche's repressive machinery. "Syntactic repression," notes Kristeva (1980, p. 278), provides the dynamic "grid" for all language systems; early desires and primitive wishes become manifest and apparent only through syntactic liberties in discourse, or lexical slips that offer opportunities for observation into internal primeval fantasy. It is on this conceptual grid that we have placed the use of a second language, having amply noted within this volume the multiple, varied, and compound uses served by a second set of symbols in the parallel elaboration and condensation and repression of personal expression (see Chapter 3). Writings from the psychoanalytic domain have further detailed the nature of linguistic repressive mechanisms, positioning general language operations and bilingual operations in particular square in the middle of the human psyche's quest for equilibrium (Freud 1900) in the face of disturbing inner conflict. The works of Greenson (1950), Kraph (1955), Buxbaum (1949),

---

10. Kristeva has described her interests in both the representational and external dimensions of speech in her dual elaboration of *la parole* and *la langue* positions (1989).

Marcos and colleagues (1973a,b, 1976, 1977, 1979), Javier (1989, 1995, 1996), and Pérez Foster (1992, 1993a, 1994, 1996a,b,d) all mark the myriad ways in which dual-language ability is creatively used in the service of obfuscating discomfort, anxiety, and potential psychic disintegration. Thus we observe the clever use of dual-language functioning as it jockeys to isolate the painful segments of memory, dissociate the devastating events of early trauma, or create with new idiomatic symbols a self that is fresh, new, and untainted by the significations of the mother tongue.

Psycholinguistic Perspectives

Adding to the textural complexity of our understanding of bilingual processes in the psyche are discourses that were introduced in Part I of this book and that emerge from psycholinguistics and cognitive science. These perspectives pose yet another grid from which to understand dual-language processes. From the review of psycholinguistic literature in Chapter 3, we note that bilingualism has been considered from the perspective of how two languages are cortically represented in the brain and interact in cognitive processes. In early work, linguists saw a strict distinction between two different types of bilingual speakers (Ervin and Osgood 1954, Lambert et al. 1958). They viewed compound bilinguals, who had learned their languages simultaneously during childhood, as possessing a single set of representational/conceptual meanings for which the individual simply possessed two different sets of language symbols. Coordinate bilinguals, on the other hand, who had learned their two languages at different points in development within different environmental contexts, possessed separate conceptual/representational meaning systems for each language (Grosjean 1982). These latter observations advanced the idea that coordinate bilinguals possessed dual ideational systems. The relevance of this for clinicians was that a coordinate bilingual's experiences negotiated through one language code, would presumably be represented and symbolized as such in memory. Each language-specific ideational system contained its own stream of special associations, idiosyncratic meanings, and particular affective accompaniments (Kolers 1968, Marcos 1976). More prevalent perspectives today no longer subscribe to such a strict distinction between compound and coordinate bilingual speakers. Linguists now espouse the idea of a significant degree of active interdependence between the bilingual's language systems, and the notion of partially compound and partially coordinate systems in all dual-language speakers (Albert and Obler 1978). For coordinate bilinguals, writers such as Paradis (1978, 1980b), and Durgunoglo and Roediger (1987) thus propose varying and dynamic degrees of interaction or associative links between language stores of basic conceptual meaning and stores of specific meanings that are unique for each language.

For the clinician, the relative interaction of each of the bilingual's language systems is a fascinating conundrum for speculation, calling to the fore what I view as a potential intersection of both the psychoanalytic and cognitive-psycholinguistic discourses presented here. I would propose, given the bilingual speaker's relative valence, if you will, toward separations in linguistic organization, and the human tendency toward psychic repression of conflictual experience, that these two vectors probably interact in a confounding manner under conditions of emotional conflict and distress. Thus language-specific experiences, depending on their degree of conflictual valence, may or may not become consciously accessible to the alternate language system. Traversing the discursive waters of cognitive science and psychoanalysis, I am proposing that in the case of a bilingual's dual ideational systems, the associative links between these systems may be inhibited by psychic repressive mechanisms. Of clear interest to the clinician here, then, are the segments of language-specific experience that could be potentially repressed, that is, operationally dissociated from conscious involvement, simply through use of an alternate language.

Blending Perspectives from Cognitive Science and Psychodevelopmental Models

Adding yet another conceptual perspective to the operation of bilingualism is work that has emerged both from cognitive science and psychodynamic exploration of the way self experiences are represented in the psyche. In Chapter 5, I discussed the idea of a *bilingual self.* This was my description of what I consider to be one of the most fascinating psychodynamic functions served by dual-language ability. I proposed that each of the bilingual's languages can serve as "characterological organizers." Into those constructs from psychoanalytic theory that maintain that people psychically internalize repeated patterns of being with an important other (Fairbairn 1952, Mitchell 1991), I integrated the early cognition work of Bartlett (1932) and others who pioneered the notion of schematic models of memory organization. The basic idea of memory as schema has been developed and applied by many cognitive researchers. Applicable to our interests here are the works of Schank and Abelson (1977), Rosch (1978), Singer and Salovey (1988), and Bonnano (1990), who noted that the memory system, in order to accommodate the voluminous amounts of incoming experiential stimuli, for the purposes of economy organizes and schematizes experiences into categories, scripts, or prototypical units of knowledge. Bucci (1997) adds that pivotal to this schema notion, is the view of memory as a dynamic and active process that is constantly reforming and integrating new experiential elements into prototypic schema for affective, behavioral, and cognitive operations that have been established throughout the developmental trajectory. Through episodic repetitions of singularly experienced or jointly experienced affective states with primary others across time, children in early development begin to construct prototypic experiential schemas. These states are accompanied by sensorial, visceral, and motoric elements, and, later in the symbolic period, are enjoined by verbal symbol elements as well—that is, language (Bucci 1997, Stern 1985). Concrete episodic events which are experienced with another and accompanied by consistent affective, visceral, sensorial, motoric, and later linguistic elements are schematized as such, laid down in memory, and provide an internalized representation of prototypic self-states. This internalized self-state holds the contingencies, so to speak, for a particular state of the self interacting with an important other, including how to perceive the other, what to expect, and how to behave with them (Bucci 1997). The establishment of these schemas is probably best represented by Stern's (1985) concept of *representations of interactions that have been generalized* (RIGs) by the early infant. His proposition is that the adult's internalized emotion schemas are based on repeated interactions with early primary figures and the emotional valences which consistently circumscribed those relationships. Clinically, we are most familiar with these developmental phenomena in transferential evocations. From a clinical perspective, Luborsky and Crits-Cristoph (1990) developed a similar schematizing concept in their "core conflictual relationship theme" (p. 10), noting the reported emergence of emotion schema in adult object relationships and the clinical transference.

Bucci (1997), in her elaboration of a multiple-code theory for explaining human information processing operations, proposes a three-channel system through which experience is encoded and internalized in the psyche. Noting the *presymbolic* (visceral, sensorial, perceptual), *imagistic*, and *verbal* channels for codifying and processing experience, she highlights the dynamic interaction of these multiple channels, their functional involvement in establishing self-related schema, and their capacity for interactive arousal in the presence of an activating contingency. Thus "any component [channel] that is activated has the potential to activate other elements such that language or imagery may activate traces of sensory or visceral experience or action; or the converse" (Bucci, p. 199). Similarly, in the case of Stern's (1985) RIG schema, a visceral state, for example, that is prototypically aligned with particular sensorial images or word representations, when aroused, can stimulate a reverberative cascade of arousal throughout that schema. An older child feeling visceral pangs of hunger could experience a familiar prototypic state laid down in early life that was schematized along with accompanying verbal negations and images of aloneness.

In earlier papers in which I introduced the notion of the bilingual self, I proposed that self schemas internalized through specific verbal codes could be both easily evoked and similarly avoided, that is, dissociated or repressed, through respective use or disuse of the language code in which these early prototypic interactions with another were experienced, codified, and internalized. As part of prototypical self-schema, language provides broad signifying functions and arousal potentials. According to Bucci's information-processing model (1997), language can activate self schema through presymbolic channels (e.g., the tones and cadence of language evoking particular ways of feeling and "being"), as well as through verbal channels, where language-related word meanings would likewise arouse a particular language-related self state. For the clinician then, the ability to engage the patient in treatment through the language in which certain internalized self-schema were codified would certainly be of constructive use in the treatment process.

CLINICAL INTERVENTIONS AND HOPE FOR THE MONOLINGUAL CLINICIAN

Viewed from a systemic perspective, I have traversed multiple bio-psycho-social domains of academic exploration in the effort to understand the dynamics of bilingual language ability in the psyche, and most particularly in the way this capacity impacts on clinical phenomena. While there are those who may disagree with my integration of sociocultural, psychoanalytic, cognitive, and neurolinguistic phenomena and discourses to understand the bilingual person,[11] the question for the clinician who treats

---

11. See Massey (1996) for a critique of this position, and Pérez Foster (1996b) for a response.

bilingual people is nevertheless a rather basic one. Whether emerging from the psychoanalytically informed discourses on bilingualism that argue for language-related repressive operations, or those discourses that propose language-related neurolinguistic structures, the evidence variously and compellingly moves toward showing that bilingual people manifest language differences in the cognitive organization of experience, memory reconstruction, sense of self, dissociative processes, defense formation, transference enactments, and possibly manifest pathology as well. How can the clinician who has no knowledge of the patient's first language code gain intimate access to those language-related experiences?

Guided by my academic explorations and, fortunately, by my exposure to a multiethnic client population in the New York area, my work with bilingual patients in clinical practice over the years has led me toward several interventions. My bilingual practice with Spanish/English patients in psychoanalysis has been invaluable in enlightening me on the depths of language operations within the psyche. This work in particular has made me a true believer in the power of bilingualism to both ally itself against the experience of psychic pain, and to work in transformative adaptation toward the development of new self experience. I thank these patients for showing me this.

My English monolingual work with bilingual patients whose native language I do not know has at times over the years thrown me into a cauldron of doubt and concern, making me wonder whether our English work is a "pseudotherapy" which simply sides with the patient's resistance to the mother tongue and the mother era, or a "quasitherapy" where the essential material is lost in the complex cognitive traffic of bilingualism and its ensuing impact on translation. Influenced by the rich and variegated depths of my bilingual work with Spanish/English patients, I knew of the rich stores of associations, feeling states, and specialized nuances of meaning that would stay beyond my grasp with patients whose first language I did not know. I was impatient in waiting for the occasional bilingual lexical slip which might offer me a fresh glimmer of the psychic interior. I presented my concerns and what I viewed as the therapeutic language dilemma to many of these ethnic patients, and together with some of them began the exciting process of creating new forays of observation into their dual-language worlds. I thank these particular patients for allowing me entry into their native language spaces, and helping me to create guideposts for my future work with them and others.

In the following pages I would like to simply describe various approaches that I have used, particularly with those clients whose native language I do not know. Some of these interventions have already been demonstrated in the clinical case presentations of previous chapters. Most importantly, these interventions are all informed by the multidisciplinary conceptual models and research data that I have presented throughout this book and summarized at the opening of this chapter.

Using the Psycholinguistic History

Chapter 7 delineates and describes how to take a Psycholinguistic History from a bilingual patient (see Table 7–1). This is a guided inquiry format that can render key information on the role that bilingualism played in the process of the client's psychodevelopment—specifically the role of language in the organization of their self experiences and their construction of defensive structures (Psychodevelopmental Factors). Secondly, the Psycholinguistic History also offers important information on the role of the client's two languages in the client's current psychological life (Current Usage Factors) and expressed psychopathology.

I cannot emphasize enough the wealth of information that can be gleaned by the monolingual clinician through simple inquiry into the languages that were used to negotiate and subsequently internalize various early object relations. These languages will be inextricably bound to those deep internalized relationships, and within their meanings the vicissitudes of their specific self-other configurations will be pointedly evoked. Notice whether these early languages are used in the patient's current life and relationships. If they are, what are these intimate relationships like, and do they transferentially enact problematic elements internalized from the primary objects? If the early language is not used, why is it not? Are the reasons based on the practical demands of the environment: "No one speaks Hungarian in my network of friends"; or are there also reasons of a dynamic nature, where there is a forcible attempt being made to emigrate from, disavow, and even dissociate from the traumatic experiences lived in the mother tongue: "When I finally got to the United States, I decided to forget everything from the past, to become American, and forget the Holocaust in Hungary where I lost my family." This data, collected from the Psycholinguistic History, is a fairly clear statement of second-language usage in the service of defensive splitting off of overwhelming affect.

For the person who has acquired a second language along the trajectory of their development, inquire into the ego capacities (e.g., new academic abilities), coping functions (e.g., assertive problem-solving behavior), and fresh, language-related affective states that were developed through the newly acquired language. Was there a language-related self-schema that evolved along with the new language and became internalized? These phenomena are graphically displayed in the cases of Anna, Yulie, and Jan, who determinedly integrated the new self experiences of their new ethnic lives to organize new self schema. Note also the facile use of a second language to encapsulate and isolate affective experience during childhood. Use the Psycholinguistic History to track differential language use as it operates in the service of coping with early trauma. For example, in the case of 13-year-old Jean Claude (see below), while he spoke to his mother in English, he was able to stave off and repress the deep longing, rage, and sense of abandonment that he experienced upon her migration to the United States. It was in his native Haitian Creole that these issues were clearly conscious, and accompanied by formidable enactments of his early trauma.

Working with Linguistic Isolation of Affect

Assuming balanced bilingual proficiency, the ability of one language code to isolate, denude, or repress the full cognitive and affective complement of a reconstructed traumatic experience that was "lived" in another language is impressive. This is noted for lived experiences in both of the bilingual's languages (not just for the mother language) (Javier et al. 1993). Notwithstanding the duly noted repressive functions that may be in operation in the case of reconstructing a conflictual event in the alternate language, there is also the body of evidence which maintains the presence of dual-language systems, such that specialized language-related elements of experience that are coded in each respective language are maintained separately. Aside from defensive psychodynamic factors, there is thus some question as to the fullness of reconstructed experience when it has been retrieved through the alternate language system (Laren 1997). In the service of obfuscating disturbing and conflictual experience that is held in the bilingual's memory, repressive and psycholinguistic vectors do seem to join forces!

For these reasons, in the case of early developmental material that I recognize to be fundamental to the dynamics of the bilingual patient, I often encourage the recounting of these experiences in the native language in which they transpired. I then have the patient simply translate the narrative to me. The level of affect and experiential depth that this can evoke for the client is quite striking. Furthermore, this intervention often stimulates a host of fresh associations which are now retrievable through the language system in which they were coded and stored. These newly evoked associations can now be translated into the language of the treatment.

I use the technique of "native language narrative followed by interpretation" for events that are of a recent nature as well. Thus a patient's account of being fired by their boss, a confrontation with their rebellious adolescent, or the deep humiliation of a verbally abusive argument with a partner, when recounted in the language of the original interchange, will tend to stimulate more experiential detail and affective arousal than if the events were recounted solely in an alternate language removed from the original experience (Javier et al. 1993, Laren 1997, Rozensky and Gomez 1983). While optimal elaboration of these events would probably take place in the therapeutic dyad which used the client's native language, the evoked affective arousal provides rich and pertinent material nevertheless for integration into the second-language treatment.

Dreams and Internal Fantasy

I often treat the recounting of dreams and the telling of internal conscious fantasy in a similar way, when these experiences have occurred in the patient's first language. Clinicians have traditionally used accounts of the patient's dream life as opportunistic entrées into the dynamics of the patient's unconscious inner landscape. When these dreams use the verbal symbols of the mother tongue, they tend to provide, in my experience, particularly rich psychic information. Especially informative is the native-language dream life of bilingual and bicultural individuals whose current usage of their native language is infrequent or absent, for the psychic material projected in the dream can be reflective of dynamic material that is defensively split off from conscious access in the second language. I always ask a bilingual patient about the language used in their dream, if any; and I also ask them to recount the dream and its associations in that language (whether I understand the native language or not). I find the associational yield to this approach extremely rich and trenchant (see Yulie's dream in Chapter 5); however, patients also tend to consciously resist it. The experience of divulging one's unconscious depths in the very language of one's early primitive experience can be rather denuding! In the case where a dream uses the patient's two languages, it is often fruitful to note the language-related content for information about what dynamic segments of psychic life are consistently associated with the use of a respective language.

I have found the most resistance to the client's telling and interpretation into English in the recounting of conscious fantasy and internal musings in the native language, as this thinking often contains transferential material about the therapist, or forbidden desires which are shameful, frightening, and best expressed within the intellectualized confines of the second language, if at all. I would like to note that the decision to make use of this "native language narrative followed by interpretation" is very much a function of the therapist's clinical judgment. Accepting the basic premise that the narration of experience *in the language of that experience* contains its fullest cognitive and affective complement, one must judge the patient's current capacity to tolerate potential ensuing anxiety. Titrating the use of this intervention should thus involve assessment of the client's current defensive state, transferential status, and conscious willingness to engage in a co-constructive enterprise of this type with the therapist. In situations involving a client's current state of psychic disintegration or impending psychosis, therapists who speak the client's native language sometimes deliberately avoid its use, using instead the binding and intellectualizing properties of the secondarily acquired language to forestall further cognitive or affective regression. Such a judgment would likewise apply to the native language narrative followed by interpretation intervention.

Exploring the Bilingual Self

I have proposed that, for bilinguals, language can sometimes serve as a characterological organizer. Repetitive and unique self-experiences that are negotiated in a specific language can be internalized as such, creating a self schema that is later evoked by language-specific use. Considering the self-schema construct from the perspective of the general psychic economy, its degree of conflictual valence will probably determine its level of integration or dissociation from general conscious psychic functioning. For the monolingual therapist, assessing the presence of bilingual self-states can be explored somewhat through use of the Psycholinguistic History, focusing on differential language usage throughout development, as well as on the domains of function and experience that were particular to each language. As an example, a Chinese-American bilingual adolescent may develop academic, social, and environmentally assertive skills in his English-speaking world, and yet function as the reserved, obedient, and deferential youngest son of his Chinese home. Bilingual and bicultural individuals are often quite aware of their dual selves as they very consciously shift their behavioral scripts between their immigrant and host cultures. Therapeutic inquiry and work could certainly be conducted along these lines, exploring consciously experienced conflicts and difficulties. However, in the case of deeply dissociated language-related self-states which are disavowed from conscious awareness, significant exploration of their conflictual dynamics and ultimate integration into the conscious psyche necessitates formidable analytic work with fulminant elaboration and working through of transference phenomena. In my view, this level of self integration necessitates work in a bilingual therapeutic setting.

Impact on the Transference

The client's shifting to the early language, even in the therapeutic dyad where the therapist does not know the client's first language, can have a significant dynamic impact on the clinical relational interaction. The client's use of the early language, according to the thinking that has been developed here (Bucci 1997, Pérez Foster 1996a,b) can evoke the arousal of self schema that in this case are language-related. Uttering one's native speech in its sensual prosody and cadence, and articulating the language-specific words that circumscribe the succinct meanings of original experience, can arouse early internalized schema of self–other experiences that can shift the vector of the clinical transference. Note my observation of the transference (and countertransference) shift in the case of Jan, after he begins to introduce his native Swedish into the treatment (see Chapter 7). While I believe that these language-related schema and transferential states are optimally maintained in treatments where use of a native language can be sustained across time (see the cases of Yulie and Anna in Chapter 5), brief evocation of these states through a native phrase or name can sometimes stimulate affective and imagistic arousals powerful enough to remain in productive play within the relational field of the treatment.

Treating Immigrant Children

Typical of the client populations that we see in agency settings are the large numbers of children who have emigrated to the United States with their families. These children are likely to learn English at a much faster pace than their parents, given concentrated exposure to school and peer settings. However, their very early developmental object experiences were negotiated in a native language, and they often continue to use that language in the native ethnic environments of their homes. Thus a split is created between native language life at home with their primary objects, and as noted in the section just above, English-speaking life at school and in the community where new social, academic, recreational, and developmental phase-specific emotional experiences are now negotiated in the new second language. The complexities of bilingualism in the academic setting are numerous, as are the factors involved in a bilingual child's cognitive development. These issues are amply treated elsewhere (Hakuta 1986, Jarvis et al. 1995). However, the language-related psychodynamic issues involved in the bilingual child's psychotherapeutic treatment are rarely examined. My involvement with immigrant Spanish-English bilingual children in treatment has led me toward phase- and context-specific use of language with the child. This is to say that, given the child's current use of English within his or her peer and school worlds, I use this language in the therapeutic inquiry and the working through of much material. This is the language of the child's currently evolving self, and the idiom through which important ego functions are being elaborated. Coasting on the momentum of their current development, bilingual immigrant children push to problem solve, explore their feelings, and elaborate their manifest fantasies in their secondarily acquired language. While second-language use may also serve to avoid early experience codified in the native idiom, the English of current life is the language code through which a tremendous range of new affective, cognitive, imagistic, and behavioral functions are being articulated. These phase- or development-specific functions are being codified and internalized in the new language. Thus, in the treatment situation, this particular material stands to be best reconstructed and worked through in that language.

The native language becomes of use, however, in the work with primary object relations and/or developmental experiences that may have taken place in the native country. These are fundamental points in the child's psychic life which still reverberate within the intimate life of home. An interesting thing that I have noticed in the common patter that children engage in during fantasy play in session is that the patter is sometimes in their native language, despite their insistence on conducting the therapeutic dialogue in their new English. For my Spanish-English young clients, these language cues are obviously easy for me to follow, as I can usually interweave the Spanish verbal narrative with the enacted play action. However, in the case of a young child whose native language I do not know, the play action provides a fruitful entrée into the patter of interior life, so to speak, rendering my lack of comprehension of the native language well compensated by the rich symbolic language of play activity.

Winnicott (1971) was wise indeed to use play in his work with adult clients, realizing its capacity for fresh, spontaneous, and creative expression that was unencumbered by the constrictions and injunctions of everyday speech. Assisted by the "play language" of children whose native language I do not speak, I feel far more hopeful of entering and understanding primary worlds of experience that are unfettered by the linguistic and psychodynamic encumbrances of second-language functioning. I seem to be making a case here for using "play language" as well with adult bilingual clients, especially those whose native idioms will never be open to my understanding. I must first work on my courage to do this, maybe enlisting my bilingual child clients for help along the way!

The Case of Jean Claude

Jean Claude was a 13-year-old Haitian boy who I saw in both individual and subsequent joint treatment with his mother. His well-turned-out homeboy look—low-hung baggy pants, backward baseball cap, untied clunky sneakers, and cool swagger, belied a deep-feeling boy who had spent years in Haiti yearning for his mother. Jean Claude was bilingual in Haitian Patois and English. He had arrived in New York at age 11 after a five-year separation from his mother, who had come to the United States to find employment and a new life for herself and her son. As is frequently seen with many Caribbean women who leave island homes for better economic and personal horizons in the United States (Pérez Foster 1998), Ms. L. had left her son in the care of her own mother. She sent money home, called monthly, and promised to send for him "soon." Jean Claude and his family lived in a particularly devastated province of rural Haiti where drought, political unrest, and a deprived economy rendered farms unworkable.

Jean Claude learned English quickly—within about a year of his arrival in the United States. He had started school with a level of enthusiasm. He was well-liked, eager to learn, and made several friends. This mood began to wane, however, approximately ten months after his arrival. He became increasingly withdrawn and was beginning to ignore his schoolwork. His teacher described him as preoccupied and day-dreamy in class. Ms. L. had her own concerns about Jean Claude. She found him distant, unaffectionate, and using English with her even when spoken to in Patois. This was viewed as a sign of disrespect. He was ungrateful, she said, for his new home, and not happy at finally being reunited with her. She was worried that there was something very wrong with him.

When Jean Claude began to see me, he was as sullen as everyone had predicted. His attitude and swagger, however, were totally undone by a round, smooth-skinned face that looked like it belonged to a handsome toddler. His English was impressively proficient, but he spoke sparingly to me, preferring instead to poke around the office playroom. His approach to me evolved into disinterested interest, and eventually he began to feel a bit freer in session. He answered very few of my questions other than how he had gotten to New York. But he did allow me to join in his fantasy play, albeit as a "stagehand" in the beginning, shifting and locating props for his "stories." He settled on many forms of innovative and creative play in which he wove narratives about superheroes taking over large cities, dinosaurs replacing all the people in the world, and emergency vehicles coming to the rescue of people and children trapped underneath the rubble of broken buildings. For a while he settled on the Lego table, building tall structures under which he put "MATCHBOX" cars, small toys, or baseball cards laid out face-up. These would be crushed by his falling Lego buildings at the end of every session. Jean Claude usually engaged in quiet, sporadic bursts of patter during his play—all of which was in Patois. He would slyly look at me at times, as if challenging me to engage with him. So I decided to in fact do that—but in English. I simply described or narrated the play action that I saw.

Jean Claude entered the doll corner one day—which he had concertedly avoided for months—and brought every doll in the collection over to the Lego table. He then began the usual game of building, destruction, and the crushing of things underneath. Thus in three-language interplay—Patois and play language (Jean Claude) and English (me)—we began the narrative reconstruction of Jean Claude's years in Haiti while he waited for his mother. He believed that he had lost her, he lacked real protection from his loving but frail grandmother, and the encroaching devastation of the countryside had created protest and violence in his town. Houses had been burned and buildings were razed for reasons inexplicable to a frightened child of 6 to 11 years. This was a depressed and traumatized boy. I asked him if his mother knew of all that he had seen while she was away. He emphatically said no.

On a day when Jean Claude, his mother, and I were discussing some practical arrangements for after-school activities, he asked his mother to stay in session so she could "see the stuff I build." We all agreed and here began a fascinating phase of the treatment in which the mother soon replaced me in narrating the play action. However, it was in Patois. We continued to work this way over several months. Ms. L. would stay in session upon invitation from Jean Claude. Slowly he began to engage her in the story of his life while he was away from her.

The clinical work now shifted to working with the mother–child dyad. Mother and son would often translate for me, but eventually it was unnecessary, as they were finally engaged in the essential discourse of their relationship, and the intimate language-world Jean Claude would need to work through his traumatic separation. Jean Claude's creative use of language in session—and his method of dealing with my "language problem"—was intriguing, uniquely adaptive, and moving. This boy had no question about the symbolic and sensual language world to which he needed to return, in order to heal himself!

12

Treating the Bilingual Patient: A Practical Guide

Given the array of multidisciplinary information and case examples that have been covered in this book, I would like to construct a practical guide for clinicians who treat bilingual ethnic clients, and cue the guide to further clinical information in the book. The brief guide is divided into two sections, which span the two broad categories of clinicians who might treat bilingual clients. Section I offers Guidelines for Clinicians with No Knowledge of the Client's Native Language, and Section II offers Guidelines for Bilingual Clinicians Who Speak the Client's Native Language.

I. GUIDELINES FOR CLINICIANS WITH NO KNOWLEDGE OF THE CLIENT'S NATIVE LANGUAGE

When Your Client Has No Command of English

1. The recommendation of choice in this situation is assessment and treatment in the client's native language. If this type of assessment is not accessible, the monolingual clinician should consider use of a translator for the assessment. This should not be a family member and should preferably be a trained mental-health translator. If this is not available, the choice should be a neutral party who the clinician can direct with the following guidelines: use of the first person (they are speaking in the voice of the

client), and use of verbatim translation. The clinician must remember to use the translator as simply a functional tool in the room, maintaining interpersonal and clinical rapport with the patient at all times. The clinician should face the client, not the translator, and maintain close eye contact with the client (see pp. 127–145).

2. In making a clinical assessment, all presenting symptoms must be understood in the context of their cultural meaning (see p. 87). The patient's expression of psychological distress should also be considered in the context of his or her being in the presence of a foreigner or stranger who may also be viewed as a member of the social group in power (see p. 93).

3. I do not favor psychotherapeutic treatment through the use of a translator.

When Your Client Has Poor Command of English

1. The recommendation of choice in this situation is for both assessment and treatment to occur in the patient's native language. When this is not a possibility and treatment will be pursued in the client's second language, it is desirable to have at least a clinical assessment which uses both of the patient's languages. Given the reported variability of symptomatic presentation that exists as a function of language, monolingual clinicians, whether they are able to avail themselves of bilingual assessment or not, must remain alert to the shifts in language-related symptom presentation that can occur (see pp. 89–90, 93).

2. Significantly influencing the presentation of the nonproficient English speaker are the struggles of translation and the efforts exerted on *how* to say things versus how one *feels* about what one is saying. Struggles with limited vocabulary may produce a dissonance between the client's narrative content and his or her emotional expres-

siveness (see pp. 86–87). Adding to the impact of these translation efforts on affective expression are the more psychodynamically driven tendencies to use the second language as a defensive isolator of deep affect. Bilinguals can sometimes efficiently split off the charged elements of early experience when they recount them in the second language. In addition, from a cognitive perspective, clinicians should be aware that there is some question concerning potential limitations in the reconstruction of experience coded and stored in a language other than that of the current treatment (see pp. 99–101). This factor also applies for balanced bilingual speakers.

3. In making their assessments, clinicians should inquire about the cultural meanings that patients may be ascribing to their symptoms, and should explore how such symptoms would be understood and treated in the patient's homeland (see pp. 86–87, 89–90).

4. Faced with treating a client who has a poor command of English, the clinician who does not speak the client's native tongue often experiences anxiety, discomfort, and feelings of inadequacy at not being able to communicate with the patient. If the therapist is able to tolerate this subjective state without the defensive tendency to disavow it, judicious self-disclosure to the patient can become part of the working therapeutic field and create potentially new areas of intersubjective connection with the patient (who of course "lives" the therapist's vulnerable experience every moment of their own day in the English-speaking world). Actively paralleling the relational aspects of the therapeutic work are the clinician's interventions, which can help to facilitate narrative reconstruction. These include encouraging the patient to recount both historical and developmental information and current experiences in the native language, then asking for a translation into English. The aim here is to access ele-

ments of language-related experience that may be coded and stored in the native language (see pp. 205–207).

When Your Client Has Proficient Command of English

1. A patient's proficient command of the therapist's language, while obliterating most of the intervening effects of translation, does not mitigate against the impact of bilingualism on the organization of psychic experience, nor the manifest expression of that experience. The clinician in this situation who is enjoying the interactive fluency of the common-language interchange in the treatment is probably the one to be most at risk in siding with the patient's potential ability to defensively use the second language to isolate disturbing elements of affective experience lived in the first language. This can become a type of language-related resistance in the treatment that has not been well documented aside from the work of the authors cited in this volume (see pp. 89–90, 95). Furthermore, the clinician must also not assume that the usual working-through of defensive resistances is all that is necessary for the reconstruction of early trauma in the bilingual because, given the influences of language-specific coding and memory storage, recall in an alternate language may influence the narrative reconstruction.

2. The patient's English fluency and presumed acculturation to American social values can likewise belie the trenchant influence of their native culture in both the construction and meaning of symptom expression. Clinicians must remain acutely aware of their own cultural countertransference on this latter issue, using caution when diagnosing as idiosyncratic pathology symptoms that may in fact be culturally syntonic behavior (see pp. 153–168).

3. The use of the Psycholinguistic History is especially im-

portant for the clinician working with the proficient English speaker, for this clinician is most likely to dismiss the impact of bilingualism on the patient's general psychodynamic operations, as noted above. Thus, directly inquiring into the object relationships and psychodevelopmental contexts within which each respective language acquisition took place will begin to introduce the clinician to the role that each language has come to play in the client's psychic processes, character formation, and defensive functions (see pp. 94–98). Language-related self-schema and potentially dissociated segments of self experience can also be discerned from this inquiry, especially when integrated with information about the transference projections and functional activities that consistently accompany each language's current usage (see pp. 105–108).

4. The following interventions can provide helpful entrée into language-related affect states and self schemas, and also evoke elements of language-related transference phenomena. From a cognitive perspective, they may also evoke arousal of experiences that were coded, stored, and schematized in that language (see pp. 197–198). 1(a) Bilingual clients should be encouraged to recount developmental and traumatic experiences in their native language to the monolingual therapist, and then simply asked to translate. (b) Dreams and fantasies, as well as current or charged experiences negotiated in the native language, can likewise be simply translated to the therapist (see pp. 205–207). In addition to stimulating new language-specific memory reconstruction, affect states, and potential transference enactments, these interventions also provide a powerful influence on the therapeutic relationship, where therapist and patient co-experience new points of connection that can serve to further deepen the clinical work (see pp. 201–213).

II. GUIDELINES FOR BILINGUAL CLINICIANS WHO SPEAK THE CLIENT'S NATIVE LANGUAGE

When Your Client Has No Command of English

1. In both assessment and treatment contexts, the client who has no command of English is clearly best served by the clinician who speaks the client's native language. Elements of the Psycholinguistic History will still be important in discerning the motivations and fantasies associated with the client's present stay in or move to the United States, and their feelings about acquiring the language of the host country. Do they intend to learn the host language? What is their experience of self while acquiring it? In what contexts do they intend to use it? What does speaking in the host language mean to them? If they have not acquired English after a stay in this country, what meaning does this have for them? Aside from these language-relevant inquiries, the treatment of a client in his or her native language obviously proceeds like any other.

2. Treating a patient in his or her native language can pose subjective issues for the bilingual therapist that related to the therapist's own language-related countertransference. The clinician who is using his or her own developmental language with an ethnically matched patient must be alert to the language-related affects and possible self-related schema that will be evoked (in the therapist), manifesting in potential transferences toward the client. Particularly notable are reactions in therapists whose language proficiency may not be as developed or sophisticated as the native client's, or the formidable reactions that can be evoked for therapists who have maintained a significant split between their native language self (and all of its associated vicissitudes) and their English-language, Americanized, professional self (see pp. 185–191).

   Clinicians who are conducting a treatment in what is

for them a secondarily acquired language must also be alert to their own countertransferential issues in speaking with a possibly more proficient native. Also, what does use of this new language mean to the therapist? What aspects of themselves does the language evoke, validate, or express? A self that is more emotional, intellectual, sensual, sophisticated, politically correct, closer to the common man or woman?

When Your Client Has Dual-Language Proficiency

1. The optimal clinical situation for any bilingual patient who integrates current usage of their respective languages in daily life is probably a bilingual treatment context with a bilingual clinician. This holds for bilinguals at varying levels of second-language proficiency, because this particular therapeutic context has at its disposal the wide spectrum of psychodynamic processes that may have been influenced by bilingual ability; for example, ego functions, defense formation, and self-organizations. In addition, internalized object-relations will render themselves more available to deep exploration in a bilingual treatment, as the therapeutic dyad's capacity to use both of the client's languages will permit resonant and trenchant development of transference phenomena (see pp. 71–75, 99).

2. Assessment of symptomatology should span use of both languages, given the variance that is known to occur as a function of the language of evaluation (see p. 99). Initial detailed use of the Psycholinguistic History inquiry for both languages will yield important developmental data, particularly in the areas of object relations, ego operations, and self organizations (see pp. 105–108). However, the dyad's dual-language ability will permit active language-switching within the treatment, which initially, when driven by the patient, will provide rich information on the use of language in psychodynamic processes. The thera-

pist can also make judicious use of language switching as a quasi-interpretive intervention, given the capacity of language to evoke language-specific material that has been coded in sensorial and/or verbal channels of information storage.

References

Abramowitz, S. I., and Murray, J. (1983). Race effects in psychotherapy. In *Bias in Psychotherapy*, ed. J. Murray and P. Abramson, pp. 215–255. New York: Praeger.

Albert, M. L., and Obler, L. K. (1978). *The Bilingual Brain: Neuropsychological and Neurolinguistic Aspects of Bilingualism*. New York: Academic Press.

Altman, N. (1993). Psychoanalysis and the urban poor. *Psychoanalytic Dialogues* 3:29–50.

——— (1995). *The Analyst in the Inner City*. Hillsdale, NJ: Analytic Press.

Amati-Mehler, J., Argentieri, S., and Canestri, J. (1993). *The Babel of the Unconscious*. Madison, CT: International Universities Press.

Anzieu, D. (1983). La evoltura sonora del sí. In *Narcisismo*, ed. G. Rosolata, A. Green, D. Anzieu, and M. Khan, pp. 59–78. Buenos Aires: Ediciones del 80.

Aragno, A., and Schlachet, P. J. (1996). Accessibility of early experience through the language of origin: a theoretical integration. *Psychoanalytic Psychology* 13:23–34.

Aron, L. (1990). One-person and two-person psychologies and the method of psychoanalysis. *Psychoanalytic Psychology* 7:475–485.

——— (1991). The patient's experience of the analyst's subjectivity. *Psychoanalytic Dialogues* 1:29–51.

Atkinson, D. R. (1985). A meta-review of research on cross-cultural counseling and psychotherapy. *Journal of Multicultural Counseling and Development* 1:138–153.

Baker, N. (1981). Social work through an interpreter. *Social Work* 26:391–397.

Bakhtin, M. (1981). *The Dialogic Imagination*, ed. M. Holquist, trans. C. Emerson and M. Holquist. Austin, TX: University of Texas Press.

Balkányi, C. (1964). On verbalization. *International Journal of Psychiatry* 45:66–74.

Bamford, K. W. (1991). Bilingual issues in mental health assessment and treatment. *Hispanic Journal of Behavioral Sciences* 13:377–390.

Bartlett, F. G. (1932). *Remembering*. Cambridge, England: Cambridge University Press.

Bastion, C. (1984). *A Treatise on Aphasia and Other Speech Defects*. London: Lewis.

Baxter, H., and Cheng, L. Y. (1996). Use of interpreters in individual psychotherapy. *Australian, New Zealand Journal of Psychiatry* 30:153–156.

Beebe, B., Alson, D., Jaffe, J., et al. (1988). Vocal congruence in mother–infant play. *Journal of Psychological Research* 17:245–259.

Bellak, L. (1948). *Dementia Praecox: The Past Decade's Work and Present Status*. New York: Grune & Stratton.

Berkanovic, E. (1980). The effect of inadequate language translation on Hispanics' responses to health surveys. *American Journal of Public Health* 70:1273–1276.

Bloom, L. (1973). *One word at a time: the use of single word utterances before syntax*. Hawthorne, NY: Mouton.

Bollas, C. (1987). *The Shadow of the Object*. New York: Columbia University Press.

Bonanno, G. A. (1990). Remembering and psychotherapy. *Psychotherapy: Theory, Research and Practice* 27:175–186.

Bouchard, M. A., and Guerette, L. (1991). Psychotherapy as a hermeneutical experience. *Psychotherapy* 28:285–393.

Bowie, M. (1991). *Lacan*. Cambridge, MA: Harvard University Press.

Bradford, D. T., and Muñoz, A. (1993). Translation in bilingual psychotherapy. *Professional Psychology: Research and Practice* 24:52–61.

Bromberg, P. M. (1993). Shadow and substance: a relational perspective on clinical process. *Psychoanalytic Psychology* 10:147–168.

—— (1996). Standing in spaces: the multiplicity of self and the psychoanalytic relationship. *Contemporary Psychoanalysis* 32:509–536.

Brown, J. (1972). *Aphasia, Apraxia and Agnosia: Clinical and Theoreti-*

cal Aspects. Springfield, IL: Charles C Thomas.

Brown, R. W., and Lennenberg, E. H. (1954). A study in language and cognition. *Journal of Abnormal and Social Psychology* 49:454–462.

Bruner, J. S. (1977). Early social interaction and language acquisition. In *Studies in Mother–Infant Interaction*, ed. H. R. Schaffer, pp. 19–28. London: Academic Press.

———— (1981). The social context of language acquisition. *Language and Communication* 1:155–178.

———— (1986). Value presuppositions of developmental theory. In *Value Presuppositions in Theories of Human Development*, ed. L. Cirillo and S. Wapner, pp. 19-36. Hillsdale, NJ: Lawrence Erlbaum.

Bucci, W. (1994). The multiple code theory and the psychoanalytic process: a framework for research. *Annual of Psychoanalysis* 22:239–260.

———— (1997). *Psychoanalysis and Cognitive Science.* New York: Guilford.

Bush, I. R., and Sainz, A. (1997). Preventing substance abuse from undermining permanency planning: competencies at the intersection of culture, chemical dependency and child welfare. *Journal of Multicultural Social Work* 5:79–97.

Buxbaum, E. (1949). The role of the second language in the formation of the ego and superego. *Psychoanalytic Quarterly* 18:279–289.

Cannon, C. B. (1983). Using an interpreter in cross-cultural counseling. *The School Counselor* 31:11–16.

Chary, P. (1986). Aphasia in a multilingual society: a preliminary study. In *Language Processing in Bilinguals: Psycholinguistic and Neuropsychological Perspectives*, ed. J. Vaid, pp. 183–197. Hillsdale, NJ: Lawrence Erlbaum.

Cirillo, L., and Wapner, S. (1986). *Value Presuppositions in Theories of Human Development.* Hillsdale, NJ: Lawrence Erlbaum.

Cohen, C. I. (1990). Outcome of schizophrenia into later life: an overview. *The Gerontologist* 30:790–797.

Comas-Diaz, L., and Griffith, E. (1988). *Cross-Cultural Mental Health.* New York: Wiley.

Cushman, P. (1990). Why the self is empty? Toward a historically situated psychology. *American Psychologist* 45:599–611.

———— (1991). Ideology obscured: political uses of the self in Daniel Stern's infant. *American Psychologist* 46:206–219.

———— (1995). *Constructing the Self, Constructing America*. New York: Addison Wellesley.

Davies, J. M. (1996). Linking the "pre-analytic" with the postclassical: integration, dissociation and the multiplicity of unconscious process. *Contemporary Psychoanalysis* 32:553–576.

DeCasper, A., and Fifer, W. (1980). Of human bonding: newborns prefer their mother's voices. *Science* 208:1174–1176.

Del Castillo, J. C. (1970). The influence of language upon symptomatology in foreign born patients. *American Journal of Psychiatry* 127:160–162.

Desjarlais, R., Eisenberg, L., Good, B., and Kleinman, A. (1995). *World Mental Health*. New York: Oxford University Press.

de Zulueta, F. (1990). Bilingualism in family therapy. *Journal of Family Therapy* 12:255–265.

Doi, T. (1962). Amae—a key concept for understanding Japanese personality structure. *Psychologia* 5:1–7.

Dore, J. (1975a). Holophrases, speech acts and language universals. *Journal of Child Language* 2:21–40.

———— (1975b). A pragmatic description of early language development. *Journal of Psycholinguistic Research* 4:343–351.

Durgunoglo, A., and Roediger, H. (1987). Test differences in accessing bilingual memory. *Journal of Memory and Language* 26:377–391.

Edgcumbe, R. (1981). Towards a developmental line for the acquisition of language. *Psychoanalytic Study of the Child* 36:71–103. New Haven, CT: Yale University Press.

Emde, R. N., Klingman, D. H., Reich, J. H., and Wade, J. D. (1978). Emotional expression in infancy: initial studies of social signaling and an emergent model. In *The Development of Affect*, ed. M. Lewis and L. Rosenblum. New York: Plenum.

Ervin, S. M. (1961). Learning and recall in bilinguals. *American Journal of Psychology* 74:233–241.

———— (1964). Language and T.A.T. content in bilinguals. *Journal of Abnormal and Social Psychology* 68:500–507.

Ervin, S. M., and Osgood, C. E. (1954). Second language learning and bilingualism. *Journal of Abnormal and Social Psychology* 49:139–146.

Ervin-Tripp, S. (1968). An analysis of the interaction of language, topic and listener. In *Readings in the Sociology of Language*, ed. J.

Fishman, pp. 42–63. The Hague: Mouton.

Fairbairn, W. R. D. (1952). *Psychoanalytic Studies of the Personality*. London: Routledge, 1981.

Ferenczi, S. (1911). On obscene words. In *Sex in Psychoanalysis: Contributions to Psychoanalysis*. New York: Brunner/Mazel, 1950.

Findling, J. (1969). Bilingual need affiliation and future orientation in extragroup and intragroup domains. *Modern Language Journal* 53:227–231.

Fishman, J. (1965). Who speaks what language to whom and when? *Linguistique* 2:67–88.

Flegenheimer, F. A. (1989). Languages and psychoanalysis: The polyglot patient and the polyglot analyst. *International Review of Psycho-Analysis* 16:377–383.

Freed, A. O. (1988). Interviewing through an interpreter. *Social Work* 33(4):315–319.

Freud, S. (1900). The interpretation of dreams. *Standard Edition* 4/5.

——— (1905). Three essays on the theory of sexuality. *Standard Edition* 7:125–243.

——— (1915). Papers on metapsychology. The unconscious. *Standard Edition* 14:159–217.

Frishberg, N. (1990). *Interpreting*. Silver Spring, MD: Registry of Interpreters for the Deaf Publications.

Gaines, A. (1992). Ethnopsychiatry: the cultural construction of psychiatries. In *Ethnopsychiatry*, ed. A. Gaines, pp. 3–49. Albany, NY: State University of New York Press.

Gay, P. (1988). *Freud: A Life For Our Time*. New York: Norton.

Genesee, F. (1978). Is there an optional age for starting second language instruction? *McGill Journal of Education* 13:145–154.

Gerver, D., and Sinaiko, H. W. (1978). *Language Interpretation and Communication*. New York: Plenum.

Gil, R. M., and Vazquez, C. I. (1996). *The Maria Paradox*. New York: Perigee.

Gill, M. M. (1983). The interpersonal paradigm and the degree of the therapist's involvement. *Contemporary Psychoanalysis* 19:200–237.

Glanzer, M., and Cunitz, A. R. (1966). Two storage mechanisms in free recall. *Journal of Verbal Learning and Verbal Behavior* 5:351–360.

Glasser, I. (1983). Guidelines for using an interpreter in social work. *Child Welfare* 62:468–470.

Goldstein, E. G. (1995). *Ego Psychology and Social Work Practice*. New York: Free Press.

Gonzales, J. (1977). The effects of language and culture on the assessment of psychopathology. *Dissertation Abstracts International* 38:357B.

Goodglass, H. (1983). *Assessment of Aphasia and Related Disorders*. Philadelphia: Lea and Febiger.

Gorkin, M. (1996). Countertransference in cross-cultural psychotherapy. In *Reaching Across Boundaries of Culture and Class: Widening the Scope of Psychotherapy*, ed. R. Pérez Foster, M. Moskowitz, and R. A. Javier, pp. 159–176. Northvale, NJ: Jason Aronson.

Greenberg, J. R. (1991a). Countertransference and reality. *Psychoanalytic Dialogues* 1:52–73.

———— (1991b). *Oedipus and Beyond*. Cambridge, MA: Harvard University Press.

Greenberg, J. R., and Mitchell, S. A. (1983). *Object Relations in Psychoanalytic Theory*. Cambridge, MA: Harvard University Press.

Greenson, R. R. (1950). The mother tongue and the mother. *International Journal of Psychoanalysis* 31:18–23.

Grosjean, F. (1982). *Life with Two Languages*. Cambridge, MA: Harvard University Press.

Guernaccia, P. J. (1992). The societal and organizational contexts of culturally sensitive mental health services: Findings from an evaluation of bilingual/bicultural psychiatric programs. *Journal of Mental Health Administration* 19:213–223.

———— (1993). Ataques de nervios in Puerto Rico: Culture-bound syndrome or popular illness? *Medical Anthropology* 15:157–170.

Guernaccia, P., Rivera, M., France, F., and Neighbors, C. (1996). The experiences of "ataque de nervios": towards an anthropology of emotions in Puerto Rico. *Culture, Medicine and Psychiatry* 20:343–367.

Guntrip, H. (1968). *Schizoid Phenomena, Object Relations and the Self*. New York: International Universities Press.

Hakuta, K. (1986). *Mirror of Language: The Debate on Bilingualism*. New York: Basic Books.

Halliday, M. A. (1975). *Learning How to Mean*. London: Edward Arnold.

Harris, A. (1992). Dialogues as transitional space: a rapprochement of psychoanalysis and developmental psycholinguistics. In *Relational*

Perspectives in Psychoanalysis, ed. N. Skolnick and S. Warshaw, pp. 119–145. Hillsdale, NJ: Analytic Press.

——— (1996). The conceptual power of multiplicity. *Contemporary Psychoanalysis* 32:537–552.

Hartmann, H. (1964). *Essays on Ego Psychology*. New York: International Universities Press.

Harvey, M. A. (1982). The influence and utilization of an interpreter for deaf persons in family therapy. *American Annals of the Deaf* 127:821–827.

——— (1989). *Psychotherapy with Deaf and Hard-of-Hearing Persons*. Hillsdale, NJ: Lawrence Erlbaum.

Harwood, R. L., Miller, J. G., and Irizarry, N. L. (1996). *Culture and Attachment: Perceptions of the Child in Context*. New York: Guilford.

Haugen, E. (1953). *The Norwegian Language in America*. Philadelphia: University of Pennsylvania Press.

Herron, W. G. (1977). Necessary and sufficient conditions for schizophrenia research. *Psychological Reports* 41:89–92.

Hittner, A., and Bornstein, H. (1990). Group counseling with older adults: coping with late-onset hearing impairment. *Journal of Mental Health Counseling* 12:332–341.

Hoffman, E. (1989). *Lost in Translation: A Life in a New Language*. New York: Dutton.

Hoffman, I. Z. (1983). The patient as interpreter of the analyst's experience. *Contemporary Psychoanalysis* 19:389–422.

——— (1991). Towards a social-constructivist view of the psychoanalytic situation. *Psychoanalytic Dialogues* 1:74–105.

Holden, P., and Serrano, A. C. (1989). Language barriers in pediatric care. *Clinical Pediatrics* 28:193–195.

Ibrahim, F. A. (1985). Effectiveness in cross-cultural counseling and psychotherapy: a framework. *Psychotherapy* 22:321–323.

Ingram, R. M. (1974). A communication model of the interpreting process. *Journal of Rehabilitation of the Deaf* 7:3–9.

Ishisaki, H., Nguyen, Q., and Okimoto, J. (1985). The role of culture in the mental health treatment of Indo-Chinese refugees. In *Southeast Asian Mental Health: Treatment, Prevention Services, Training and Research*, ed. T. C. Owan. Rockville, MD: National Institute of Mental Health.

232   REFERENCES

Jakobovits, L., and Lambert, W. (1961). Semantic satiation among bilinguals. *Journal of Experimental Psychology* 62:576–582.

Jarvis, L. H., Danks, J. H., and Merriman, W. E. (1995). The effect of bilingualism on cognitive ability: a test of the level of bilingualism hypothesis. *Applied Psycholinguistics* 16:293–308.

Javier, R. A. (1989). Linguistic considerations in the treatment of bilinguals. *Journal of Psychoanalytic Psychology* 6:80–96.

——— (1995). Vicissitudes of autobiographical memories in bilingual analysis. *Psychoanalytic Psychology* 12:429–438.

——— (1996). In search of repressed memories. In *Reaching Across Boundaries of Culture and Class: Widening the Scope of Psychotherapy*, ed. R. Pérez Foster, M. Moskowitz, and R. A. Javier, pp. 225–242. Northvale, NJ: Jason Aronson.

Javier, R. A., Barroso, F., and Muñoz, M. A. (1993). Autobiographical memory in bilinguals. *Journal of Psycholinguistic Research* 22:319–338.

Jenkins, J. (1994). Culture, emotion and psychopathology. In *Emotion and Culture*, ed. S. Kitayama and R. Markus, pp. 307–335. Washington, DC: American Psychological Association.

Kaul, A., Landfermann, H., and Thieme, M. (1996). One decade after Chernobyl: summing up the consequences. *Health Physics* 71:634–640.

Kim, K. H., Relkin, N. R., Lee, K. M., and Hirsch, J. (1997). Distinct cortical areas associated with native and second languages. *Nature* 388:171–174.

Kinzie, J. D. (1985). Overview of clinical issues in the treatment of Southeast Asian refugees. In *Southeast Asian Mental Health: Treatment, Prevention Services, Training and Research*, ed. T. C. Owan. Rockville, MD: National Institute of Mental Health.

Kirschner, S. (1990). The assenting echo: Anglo-American values in contemporary psychoanalytic developmental psychology. *Social Research* 57:821–857.

Kitayama, S., and Markus, H. R. (1994). *Emotion and Culture*. Washington, DC: American Psychological Association.

Klein, M. (1932). *The Psycho-Analysis of Children*. Reprinted as *The Writings of Melanie Klein*, vol. 3. London: Hogarth, 1975.

Kline, F., Acosta, F. X., Austin, W., and Johnson, R. G. (1980). The misunderstood Spanish-speaking patient. *American Journal of Psychiatry* 137:1530–1532.

Klinnert, M. D., Campos, J. J., Sorce, J. F., et al. (1983). Emotions as behavior regulators: social referencing in infancy. In *Emotion: Theory, Research and Experience*, vol. 2, ed. R. Plutchik and H. Kellerman. New York: Academic Press.

Kohut, H. (1971). *The Analysis of the Self.* New York: International Universities Press.

Kolers, P. A. (1963). Interlingual word associations. *Journal of Verbal Learning and Verbal Behavior* 2:291–300.

——— (1968). Bilingualism and information processing. *Scientific American* 218:78–86.

Kraph, E. E. (1955). The choice of language in polyglot psychoanalysis. *Psychoanalytic Quarterly* 24:343–357.

Kristeva, J. (1980). *Desire in Language.* New York: Columbia University Press.

——— (1989). *Language: the Unknown.* New York: Columbia University Press.

LaBruzza, A. L., and Mendez-Villarrubia, J. M. (1994). *Using DSM-IV: A Clinician's Guide to Psychiatric Diagnosis.* Northvale, NJ: Jason Aronson.

Lacan, J. (1977). *Écrits: a Selection.* New York: Norton.

Lambert, M., and Moore, N. (1966). Word-association responses: comparison of American and French monolinguals with Canadian monolinguals and bilinguals. *Journal of Personality and Social Psychology* 3:313–320.

Lambert, W. E. (1956). Developmental aspects of second-language acquisition: I. Associational fluency, stimulus provocativeness, and word order influence. *Journal of Social Psychology* 43:83–89.

Lambert, W., Havelka, J., and Crosby, C. (1958). The influence of language-acquisition contexts on bilingualism. *Journal of Abnormal and Social Psychology* 56:239–244.

Laren, S. (1997). *Differences in affect expression and object relations in the early memories of Spanish/English coordinate bilinguals.* Unpublished doctoral dissertation. New York: Gordon F. Derner Institute of Advanced Psychological Studies, Adelphi University.

Laski, E., and Taleporos, E. (1977). Anticholinergic psychosis in a bilingual: a case study. *American Journal of Psychiatry* 134:1038–1040.

Lesser, R. C. (1996). "All that's solid melts into air": deconstructing some psychoanalytic facts. *Contemporary Psychoanalysis* 32:5–23.

Levine, R. (1990). Infant environments in psychoanalysis: a cross-cultural view. In *Cultural Psychology: Essays on Comparative Human Development*, ed. J. Stigler, R. Schweder, and G. Herdt, pp. 454–476.

Loewald, H. (1980). Primary process, secondary process and language. In *Papers on Psychoanalysis*, ed. H. Loewald, pp. 178–206. New Haven, CT: Yale University Press.

Loewenstein, R. J., and Ross, D. R. (1992). Multiple personality and psychoanalysis: an introduction. *Psychoanalytic Inquiry* 12:3–48.

Loewenstein, R. M. (1956). Some remarks on the role of speech in psycho-analytic technique. *International Journal of Psycho-Analysis* 37:460–468.

Loftus, E. F., and Hoffman, H. G. (1989). Misinformation and memory: the creation of new memories. *Journal of Experimental Psychology* 118:100–104.

Loftus, E. F., and Klinger, M. R. (1992). Is the unconscious smart or dumb? *American Psychologist* 47:761–765.

Luborsky, L. (1988). A comparison of three transference related measures applied to the specimen hour. In *Psychoanalytic Process Research Strategies*, ed. H. Dahl, H. Kaechele, and H. Themae, pp. 109–115. New York: Springer.

Luborsky, L., and Crits-Cristoph, P. (1990). *Understanding Transference: The CCRT Method*. New York: Basic Books.

Lutz, C. (1988). *Unnatural Emotions*. Chicago: University of Chicago Press.

Lutz, C., and White, G. (1986). The anthropology of emotions. *Annual Review of Anthropology* 15:405–436.

MacKinnon, R., and Michels, R. (1971). *The Psychiatric Interview in Clinical Practice*. Philadelphia: Saunders.

Macnamara, J. (1967). The linguistic independence of bilinguals. *Journal of Verbal Learning and Verbal Behavior* 6:729–736.

Magaro, P. A. (1980). *Cognition in Schizophrenia and Paranoia: The Integration of Cognitive Processes*. Hillsdale, NJ: Lawrence Erlbaum.

Malgady, R. G., Rogler, L. H., and Constantino, G. (1987). Ethnocultural and linguistic bias in mental health evaluation of Hispanics. *American Psychologist* 42:228–234.

Malinowski, B. (1926). *Crime and Custom in Savage Society*. Totowa, NJ: Littlefield, Adams.

Marcos, L. R. (1972). Lying: a particular defense met in psychoanalytic therapy. *American Journal of Psychoanalysis* 32:195–202.

——— (1976). Bilinguals in psychotherapy: language as an emotional barrier. *American Journal of Psychotherapy* 30:552–560.

——— (1979). Effects of interpreters on the evaluation of psychopathology in non-English speaking patients. *American Journal of Psychiatry* 136:171–174.

Marcos, L. R., and Alpert, M. (1976). Strategies and risks in psychotherapy with bilingual patients. *American Journal of Psychiatry* 133:1275–1278.

Marcos, L. R., Alpert, M., Urcuyo, L., and Kesselman, M. (1973a). The effect of interview language on the evaluation of psychopathology in Spanish-American schizophrenic patients. *American Journal of Psychiatry* 130:549–553.

Marcos, L. R., Eisma, J. E., and Guimon, J. (1977). Bilingualism and the sense of self. *American Journal of Psychotherapy* 37:285–290.

Marcos, L. R., and Urcuyo, L. (1979). Dynamic psychotherapy with the bilingual patient. *American Journal of Psychotherapy* 33:331–338.

Marcos, L. R., Urcuyo, L., Kesselman, M., and Alpert, M. (1973b). The language barrier in evaluating Spanish-American patients. *Archives of General Psychiatry* 29:655–659.

Martin, G., and Clark, R. (1982). Distress crying in neonates: species and peer specificity. *Developmental Psychology* 18:3–9.

Massey, C. (1996). The cultural and conceptual dissonance in theoretical practice: commentary on RoseMarie Pérez Foster's "The Bilingual Self: Duet in Two Voices." *Psychoanalytic Dialogues* 6:123–140.

Mays, V. (1985). The Black-American and psychotherapy: the dilemma. *Psychotherapy* 22:379–387.

McDougall, J. (1989). *Theaters of the Body.* New York: Norton.

McGoldrick, M., Pearce, J. K., and Giordano, J. (1982). *Ethnicity and Family Therapy.* New York: Guiford.

Mead, M. (1935). *Sex and Temperament in Three Primitive Societies.* New York: Morrow.

Mehler, J., Jusczyk, P., Lambertz, G., Halsted, N., et al. (1988). A precursor of language acquisition in young infants. *Cognition* 29:143–178.

Menaker, E. (1989). *Appointment in Vienna.* New York: St. Martin's Press.

Mikkelson, H. (1983). Consecutive interpretation. *The Reflector* 6:5–9.

Mitchell, S. A. (1988). *Relational Concepts in Psychoanalysis*. Cambridge, MA: Harvard University Press.

——— (1991). Contemporary perspectives on self: toward an integration. *Psychoanalytic Dialogues* 1:121–148.

Nelson, K. (1990). *Narratives from the Crib*. Cambridge, MA: Harvard University Press.

Neufeld, R. W. (1977). Response-selection processes in paranoid and non-paranoid schizophrenia. *Perceptual and Motor Skills* 44:499–505.

Northcott, W. H. (1984). *Oral Interpreting Principles and Practices*. University Park, MD: University Park Press.

Obholzer, K. (1982). *The Wolf-Man Sixty Years Later*. New York: Continuum.

Ojemann, G. A. (1991). Cortical organization of language. *Journal of Neuroscience* 11:2281–2287.

Ojemann, G. A., and Whitaker, H. A. (1978). The bilingual brain. *Archives of Neurology* 35:409–412.

Olarte, S. W., and Lenz, B. (1984). Learning to do psychoanalytic therapy with inner-city populations. *Journal of the American Academy of Psychoanalysis* 12:89–99.

Oquendo, M. A. (1996). Psychiatric evaluation and psychotherapy in the patient's second language. *Psychiatric Services* 47:614–618.

Padilla, A. M., and Ruiz, R. A. (1973). *Latino Mental Health: A Review of the Literature* (DHEW Publication No. HSM 73-9143). Washington, DC: US Government Printing Office.

Paniagua, F. (1994). *Assessing and Treating Culturally Diverse Clients: A Practical Guide*. Thousand Oaks, CA: Sage.

Paradis, M. (1977). Bilingualism and aphasia. In *Studies in Neurolinguistics*, vol. 3, ed. H. Whitaker and H. Whitaker, pp. 65–121. New York: Academic Press.

——— (1978). *Bilingual Linguistic Memory: Neurolinguistic Considerations*. Paper presented at the meeting of the Linguistic Society of America, Boston, MA, November.

——— (1980a). *Language and Thought in Bilinguals. In the Sixth LACUS Forum*. Columbia, SC: Hornbeam.

——— (1980b). The language switch in bilinguals: psycholinguistic and neurolinguistic perspectives. In *Languages in Contact and Con-*

flict, ed. P. Nelde. Wiesbaden, Germany: Franz Steine Verlag.

Penfield, W., and Roberts, L. (1959). *Speech and Brain Mechanisms.* Princeton, NJ: Princeton University Press.

Pérez Foster, R. (1981). The effects of subliminal tachistoscopic presentation of drive-related stimuli on the cognitive functioning of paranoid and nonparanoid schizophrenics. *Dissertation Abstracts International* 42:10.

———— (1992). Psychoanalysis and the bilingual patient: some observations on the influence of language choice on the transference. *Psychoanalytic Psychology* 9:61–76.

———— (1993a). *The bilingual self.* Paper presented at the thirteenth annual spring meeting of the Division of Psychoanalysis of the American Psychological Association, April 17.

———— (1993b). The social politics of psychoanalysis. *Psychoanalytic Dialogues* 3:69–84.

———— (1994). *Exploring psychic duality in the bilingual patient.* Paper presented at the 14th Division 39 Spring Meeting of the American Psychological Association, Washington, DC, April 13–17.

———— (1996a). The bilingual self: duet in two voices. *Psychoanalytic Dialogues* 6:99–121.

———— (1996b). The bilingual self: notions of a scientific positivist or pragmatic psychoanalyst? *Psychoanalytic Dialogues* 6:141–150.

———— (1996c). What is a multicultural perspective for psychoanalysis? In *Reaching Across Boundaries of Culture and Class: Widening the Scope of Psychotherapy*, ed. R. Pérez Foster, M. Moskowitz, and R. A. Javier, pp. 3–20. Northvale, NJ: Jason Aronson.

———— (1996d). Assessing the psychodynamic function of language in the bilingual patient. In *Reaching Across Boundaries of Culture and Class: Widening the Scope of Psychotherapy*, ed. R. Pérez Foster, M. Moskowitz, and R. A. Javier, pp. 243–263. Northvale, NJ: Jason Aronson.

———— (1998). The clinician's cultural countertransference: the psychodynamics of culturally competent practice. *Clinical Social Work Journal* 26(3):253–270.

Pérez Foster, R., Moskowitz, M., and Javier, R. A. (1996e). *Reaching Across Boundaries of Culture and Class: Widening the Scope of Psychotherapy.* Northvale, NJ: Jason Aronson.

Price, C. S., and Cuellar, I. (1981). Effects of language and related variables on the expression of psychopathology in Mexican American psychiatric patients. *Hispanic Journal of Behavioral Sciences* 3:145–160.

Price, J. (1975). Foreign language interpreting in psychiatric practice. *Australian, New Zealand Journal of Psychiatry* 4:263–267.

Putnam, F. W. (1984). The psychophysiological investigation of multiple personality disorder. *Psychiatric Clinics of North America* 7:31–40.

——— (1988). The switch process in multiple personality disorder. *Dissociation* 1:24–32.

Racker, H. (1968). *Transference and Countertransference.* New York: International Universities Press.

——— (1988). The meanings and uses of countertransference. In *Essential Papers on Countertransference*, ed. B. Wolstein, pp. 158–201. New York: New York University Press.

Rank, O. (1945). *Will Therapy and Truth and Reality.* New York: Knopf.

Rendon, M. (1996). Psychoanalysis in an historic economic perspective. In *Reaching Across Boundaries of Culture and Class: Widening the Scope of Psychotherapy*, ed. R. Pérez Foster, M. Moskowitz, and R. A. Javier, pp. 47–70. Northvale, NJ: Jason Aronson.

Richie, J. (1964). Using an interpreter effectively. *Nursing Outlook* 12:27–29.

Roe, D. L., and Roe, C. E. (1991). The third party: using interpreters for the deaf in counseling situations. *Journal of Mental Health Counseling* 13:91–105.

Roland, A. (1988). *In Search of the Self in India and Japan.* Princeton, NJ: Princeton University Press.

——— (1996). *Cultural Pluralism and Psychoanalysis: An Asian and North American Experience.* New York: Routledge.

Rosch, E. (1978). Principles of categorization. In *Cognition and Categorization*, ed. E. Rosch and B. B. Lloyd. Hillsdale, NJ: Lawrence Erlbaum.

Ross, M. B., and Magaro, P. A. (1976). Cognitive differentiation between paranoid and nonparanoid schizophrenia. *Psychological Reports* 38:991–994.

Roy, C. B. (1992). *Interpreting Dialogue.* Burtonsville, MD: Linstok.

Rozensky, R. H., and Gomez, M. Y. (1983). Language switching in psychotherapy with bilinguals: two problems, two models, and case examples. *Psychotherapy: Theory, Research and Practice* 20:152–160.

Saari, C. (1988). Interpretation: event or process? *Clinical Social Work Journal* 16:378–390.

Sabin, J. E. (1975). Translating despair. *American Journal of Psychiatry* 132:197–199.

Sampson, E. (1988). The debate on individualism: indigenous psychologies of the individual. *American Psychologist* 43:15–22.

Sapir, E. (1929). The status of linguistics as a science. *Language* 5:207–214.

———— (1949). *Selected Writings in Language, Culture and Personality*. Berkeley: University of California Press.

Schafer, R. (1980). Action language and the psychology of the self. *Annual of Psychoanalysis* 8:83–92.

Schank, R. C., and Abelson, R. P. (1977). *Scripts, Plans, Goals, and Understanding*. Hillsdale, NJ: Lawrence Erlbaum.

Schweder, R. (1990). Cultural psychology: what is it? In *Cultural Psychology: Essays on Comparative Human Development*, ed. J. W. Stigler, R. Schweder, and G. Herdt, pp. 1–43. Cambridge, MA: Harvard University Press.

———— (1991). *Thinking Through Cultures*. Cambridge, MA: Harvard University Press.

Segalowitz, N. (1976). Communicative in competence and the nonfluent bilingual. *Canadian Journal of Behavioral Science* 8:122–131.

Shapiro, R. J., and Harris, R. (1976). Family therapy in treatment of the deaf: a case report. *Family Process* 15:83–97.

Singer, J. A., and Salovey, P. (1988). Mood and memory: evaluating the network theory of affect. *Clinical Psychology Review* 8:211–251.

Skolnick, N. J., and Warshaw, S. C. (1992). *Relational Perspectives in Psychoanalysis*. Hillsdale, NJ: Analytic Press.

Solow, S. (1981). *Sign Language Interpreting: A Basic Resource Book*. Silver Spring, MD: National Association for the Deaf.

Spence, D. P. (1982). *Narrative Truth and Historical Truth*. New York: Norton.

Stansfield, M. (1981). Psychological issues in mental health interpreting. *Registry of Interpreters for the Deaf Interpreting Journal* 1:18–31.

Stein, L. K., Mindel, E., and Jabaley, T. (1981). *Deafness and Mental Health*. New York: Grune & Stratton.

Stern, D. N. (1985). *The Interpersonal World of the Infant.* New York: Basic Books.

Stern, M. (1993). *The subjective and intersubjective experience of switching languages in analytic treatment.* Paper presented at the thirteenth annual spring meeting of the Division of Psychoanalysis, Division 39 of the American Psychological Association, April 17.

Stigler, J., Schweder, R., and Herdt, G. (1990). *Cultural Psychology: Essays on Comparative Human Development.* Cambridge, England: Cambridge University Press.

Stolorow, R. D., and Atwood, G. E. (1991). The mind and the body. *Psychoanalytic Dialogues* 1:181–196.

Sue, D. W., and Sue, D. (1990). *Counseling the Culturally Different.* New York: Wiley.

Sue, S. (1988). Psychotherapeutic services for ethnic minorities. *American Psychologist* 43:301–308.

Tannen, D. (1984). *Conversational Style: Analyzing Talk Among Friends.* Norwood, NJ: Ablex.

———— (1989). Interpreting interruption in conversation. *Proceedings of the 25th Annual Meeting of the Chicago Linguistics Society, April 28, 1984.* Chicago, IL: University of Chicago Press.

Taylor, I. (1971). How are words from two languages organized in bilinguals' memory? *Canadian Journal of Psychology / Revue Canadienne de Psychologie* 25:228–240.

Thass-Thienemann, T. (1973). *The Interpretation of Language,* vol. 1, *Understanding the Symbolic Meaning of Language.* New York: Jason Aronson.

Thompson, C. (1989). Psychoanalytic psychotherapy with inner city patients. *Journal of Contemporary Psychotherapy* 19:137–148.

———— (1996). The African-American patient in psychodynamic treatment. In *Reaching Across Boundaries of Culture and Class: Widening the Scope of Psychotherapy,* ed. R. Pérez Foster, M. Moskowitz, and R. A. Javier, pp. 115–142. Northvale, NJ: Jason Aronson.

Tomkins, S. S. (1962). *Affect, Imagery, Consciousness,* vol. 1. New York: Springer.

———— (1981). The quest for primary motives: biography and autobiography of an idea. *Journal of Personality and Social Psychology* 41:306–329.

Trevarthan, C., and Hubley, P. (1978). Secondary intersubjectivity: confidence, confiders and acts of meaning in the first year. In *Action, Gesture and Symbol*, ed. A. Lock. New York: Academic Press.

Tronick, E., Als, H., and Adamson, L. (1979). Structure of early face to face communicative reactions. In *Before speech: the beginning of interpersonal communications*, ed. M. Bullowa. New York: Cambridge University Press.

Tyler, F. B., Susswell, D. R., and Williams-McCoy, J. (1985). Ethnic validity in psychotherapy. *Psychotherapy* 22:311–320.

United States Immigration and Naturalization Service (1997). http://www.ins.usdoj.gov/stats/annual/fy96/973.html.

Urwin, C. (1984). Power relations and the emergence of language. In *Changing the Subject*, ed. J. Henriques, pp. 264–323. London: Methuen.

Vaid, J. (1986). *Language Processing in Bilinguals*. Hillsdale, NJ: Lawrence Erlbaum.

Valsiner, J. (1988). *Developmental Psychology in the Soviet Union*. Bloomington, IL: Indiana University Press.

Vazquez, C., and Javier, R. A. (1991). The problem with interpreters: communicating with Spanish-speaking patients. *Hospital and Community Psychiatry* 42:163–165.

Vazquez, C. A. (1982). Research on the psychiatric evaluation of the bilingual patient: a methodological critique. *Hispanic Journal of Behavioral Sciences* 4:75–80.

Vygotsky, L. S. (1962). *Language and Thought*. Cambridge, MA: MIT Press.

——— (1978). *Mind in Society: The Development of Higher Psychological Processes*. Cambridge, MA: Harvard University Press.

——— (1988). Thinking and speaking. In *The Collected Papers of L. S. Vygotsky*, ed. R. W. Rieber and A. S. Carton, pp. 39–288. New York: Plenum.

Weinreich, U. (1953). *Languages in Contact—Findings and Problems*. New York: Linguistic Circle of New York, Publication No. 1.

Westermeyer, J. (1987). Cultural factors in clinical assessment. *Journal of Consulting and Clinical Psychology* 55:471–478.

——— (1990). Working with an interpreter in psychiatric assessment and treatment. *Journal of Nervous and Mental Diseases* 178:745–749.

Whorf, B. L. (1956). *Language, Thought and Reality*. Cambridge, MA: MIT Press.

Wilson, A. (1989). Levels of adaptation and narcissistic pathology. *Psychiatry* 52:218–236.

Wilson, A., and Weinstein, L. (1990). Language, thought, and interiorization. *Contemporary Psychoanalysis* 26:24–40.

Winnicott, D. W. (1951). Transitional objects and transitional phenomena. In *Essential Papers on Object Relations*, ed. P. Buckley, pp. 254–271. New York: New York University Press.

———— (1965). *The Maturational Processes and the Facilitating Environment*. New York: International Universities Press.

———— (1971). *Playing and Reality*. London: Tavistock.

———— (1986). *Holding and Interpretation*. London: Hogarth.

Wolstein, B. (1988). *Essential Papers on Countertransference*. New York: New York University Press.

———— (1992). Some historical aspects of contemporary pluralistic psychoanalysis. In *Relational Perspectives in Psychoanalysis*, ed. N. J. Skolnick and S. C. Warshaw, pp. 313–331. Hillsdale, NJ: Analytic Press.

Woody, D. L. (1991). *Recruitment and Retention of Minority Workers in Mental Health Programs*. Washington, DC: National Institute of Mental Health, Human Resource Development.

Yanagida, E., and Marsella, A. J. (1978). The relationship between depression and self concept discrepancy among generations of Japanese-American women. *Journal of Clinical Psychology* 34:654–659.

Index